PRAISE FOR *THE POSTCATASTROPHE ECONOMY*

"Can America's economic potential be reached in the face of the debt deflation that Janszen describes? This book describes the financial lobbying and political interests that need to be dismantled for the economy to revive."

—MICHAEL HUDSON, DISTINGUISHED RESEARCH PROFESSOR OF ECONOMICS, UNIVERSITY OF MISSOURI, KANSAS CITY

"We need to know where we will be when we get out of this mess, and the Fed's combination of nostalgia, raw hope, and guesswork does not give much guidance. Eric Janszen, seeking scope and depth, contributes significantly to the next, necessary debate."

—MARTIN MAYER, BROOKINGS INSTITUTE GUEST SCHOLAR AND AUTHOR OF *THE FED AND THE MARKETS*

"[Janszen] has written a book suggesting how we can avoid the worst consequences of our folly as Americans struggle to pay down debt in a damaged economy. If we follow his advice, we may find alternative energy resources and increase productivity in time to become self-sustaining before the United States creates a new financial crisis that will make the current one look like a business boom."

—JANET TAVAKOLI, PRESIDENT, TAVAKOLI STRUCTURED FINANCE, AND AUTHOR OF *DEAR MR. BUFFETT*

"Eric Janszen reinforces the need to look for entrepreneurs to create new companies and new jobs, not to simply expect government economic policy to do so, and this is an all too rare perspective. Refreshing and cogent."

—BART STUCK, MANAGING DIRECTOR,
SIGNAL LAKE VENTURE PARTNERS

"Unlike the many 'told-you-so' books of the past year, Eric Janszen takes a hard look at the foundations of the Great Recession of 2009, explaining why gold prices rose, why the U.S. dollar is safer than we think, and why houses make terrible investments. And rather than suggesting another round of post-hoc regulation, Janszen points the way toward a sustainable future in infrastructure investment. Janszen has the goods."

—SCOTT REYNOLDS NELSON, LEGUM PROFESSOR OF
HISTORY, COLLEGE OF WILLIAM & MARY, AND AUTHOR
OF *CRASH: AN UNCOMMON HISTORY OF AMERICA'S
FINANCIAL DISASTERS*

"Eric Janszen gives us an eloquent and straightforward analysis of the serious challenges that face the United States today, and a prescription for how America can return to a position of greatness from an author who is optimistic and confident in the resilience and entrepreneurial spirit of the American people."

—JIM GOLDINGER, FOUNDER,
FAIRHAVEN CAPITAL PARTNERS

THE POSTCATASTROPHE ECONOMY
—

THE POSTCATASTROPHE ECONOMY

REBUILDING AMERICA AND AVOIDING THE NEXT BUBBLE

Eric Janszen

Portfolio/Penguin

PORTFOLIO / PENGUIN
Published by the Penguin Group
Penguin Group (USA) Inc., 375 Hudson Street, New York, New York 10014, U.S.A. •
Penguin Group (Canada), 90 Eglinton Avenue East, Suite 700, Toronto, Ontario, Canada
M4P 2Y3 (a division of Pearson Penguin Canada Inc.) • Penguin Book Ltd, 80 Strand,
London WC2R 0RL, England • Penguin Ireland, 25 St. Stephen's Green, Dublin 2,
Ireland (a division of Penguin Books Ltd) • Penguin Books Australia Ltd, 250
Camberwell Road, Camberwell, Victoria 3124, Australia (a division of Pearson Australia
Group Pty Ltd) • Penguin Books India Pvt Ltd, 11 Community Centre, Panchsheel Park,
New Delhi - 110 017, India • Penguin Group (NZ), 67 Apollo Drive, Rosedale, North
Shore 0632, New Zealand (a division of Pearson New Zealand Ltd) • Penguin Books
(South Africa) (Pty) Ltd, 24 Sturdee Avenue, Rosebank, Johannesburg 2196, South
Africa

Penguin Books Ltd, Registered Offices:
80 Strand, London WC2R 0RL, England

First published in 2010 by Portfolio Penguin
a member of Penguin Group (USA) Inc.

10   9   8   7   6   5   4   3   2   1

Copyright © Eric Janszen, 2010
All rights reserved

ISBN 978-1-59184-263-7

Printed in the United States of America
Set in Warnock Pro with Berthold Akzidenz Grotesk
Designed by Daniel Lagin

*For my dear, brilliant, warm, and lively wife Candy
who makes me very happy.*

CONTENTS

—

—

PART II
TECI

CHAPTER 4
The TECI Economy: Transportation, Energy, Communication,
and Infrastructure

PART III
THE MIDTERM MACRO FORECAST

CHAPTER 5
Peak Cheap Oil

CHAPTER 6
Economic and Market Forecasting in a Postbubble World

EPILOGUE

ACKNOWLEDGMENTS

INDEX

—

THE POSTCATASTROPHE ECONOMY

—

INTRODUCTION

WHAT JUST HAPPENED?

DEINDUSTRIALIZATION AND THE RISE
OF THE FIRE ECONOMY

Experience is that marvelous thing that enables you to recognize
a mistake when you make it again.

    —FRANKLIN P. JONES

Governments never learn. Only people learn.

    —MILTON FRIEDMAN

The analysis pegs the cause of the most spectacular financial crisis
ever. Published by one of the leading and most venerable economics journals in the world—the *Quarterly Journal of Economics*—the
article begins with a simple thesis, that "the existing depression was
due essentially to the great wave of credit expansion in the past decade." The author writes:

> We have undoubtedly expanded the credit structure, spending
> today and postponing the accounting until tomorrow. We have
> been guilty of the sin of inflation. . . . Credit expansion results

in business activity, in full employment, in [an] optimistic out-look and in a flood of gratulatory literature proclaiming us wiser than our predecessors. But the evidence is consistent and cumulative. The past decade has witnessed a great volume of credit inflation. Our period of prosperity in part was based on nothing more substantial than debt expansion.

The prosperity was false, built on an illusion, on the expansion of credit and inflating asset prices. The people are suddenly poorer, and appear set to stay that way for the duration. But the author sees a bright spot: For once, we will have learned our lesson. He goes on:

> When the accounts are footed we shall have learned new les-sons respecting the evils of credit inflation. This dear bought wisdom we may place beside our knowledge of the evils of mon-etary inflation purchased at an equally dear price. And we may venture a pious hope that the joint lessons will induce growth of the wisdom to foresee, caution to move less rapidly and more surely in the path of progress.

Economist Charles E. Persons penned these hopeful words in No-vember 1930, in the early years of the worst financial crisis the world had ever seen. Despite Persons's optimism, recent events inform us that we have in fact learned nothing except how to blunt the impact of the inevitable consequence of the repeated mistake of allowing a credit bubble to develop, of financial and economic catastrophe. Today, after the collapse of credit bubbles, we fight the subsequent carnage with radical government intervention in the markets and the economy.

Yet the prescription of government borrowing to reinflate the markets and the economy, while it alleviates many immediate symp-toms that a credit collapse visits upon the nation that offended forgot-ten economic law, creates new risks. History also teaches the lesson that no level of fresh borrowing or higher taxation absolves a nation of its original credit-bubble sin. Grievous consequences persist for years, or even decades, over the protests of politicians and economists who proclaim that all is well, or at least on the mend. Yet true recovery requires the nation to change its ways. Sacrifices must be made to undo the deed.

We've experienced our second credit catastrophe in one hundred years, far greater and more destructive than the last, but far more effectively managed, at least in the short run. This time the wall of debt was twenty-seven years in the making, not only nine as in the 1920s, and its structure is a complex fabric of interwoven credit relationships, a global network of financial interdependencies so intricate that the experts who created them could not determine how to separate the worthy from the worthless, the real from the imagined, the self-destructing from the yet to be destroyed. The entire economic system has been glued together by one profound fantasy: Finance can substitute for production, and credit for savings.

Private debt, of households and businesses, and public debt, of governments federal, state, and local, foreign and domestic, piled up like snow by a blizzard of lending through mortgages, bonds offerings, and securitizations over decades. It then avalanched upon us, flattening our cities and towns, burying malls, stores, and homes, entombing universities and schools, and smothering dreams. All that was solid—if not always beautiful, then at least familiar—was swept away or covered up, not only in America but around the world.

During the boom, shopping malls, casinos, and office buildings bloomed in deserts, among forests of palms and along secluded rocky shores. Today they brood, dark against the dusk, half finished, like skeletons of dinosaurs killed off in a climatic disaster. But this disaster was man-made, not natural in the least.

Tumbleweeds bounce across cracked driveways; dust blows across the dried-out brown lawns and fills the empty swimming pools of abandoned homes in Bakersfield and Yuba.

Shoddily built "luxury" condominium complexes crumble in working-class neighborhoods across South Florida once slated by real estate agents to become the Next Big Thing.

A dozen miles of shuttered toy and electronics factories line the banks of the Pearl River in Guangdong, China; thousands of businesses small and large have shut down across Europe; oil refineries fall silent in the United States.

Legions of unemployed grow by millions every month, in every nation.

And everywhere debt—mortgage debt, credit card debt, automobile loans, student loans, commercial loans. And debt paper—municipal bonds, junk bonds, bonds issued to finance schools, roads, fire stations, and a thousand other projects. And always the unpaid bills—medical, insurance, child care, heating oil or gas, taxes. Unpaid pensions. Unpaid state taxes.

Driven by consumption, the errors of credit overexpansion made in the 1920s, and before that in the 1870s, were repeated in the 1980s, 1990s, and early 2000s, but with the grim efficiency of modern financial engineering and an inevitable result—an equally efficient collapse. The river of credit-based money that had lifted many lives washed back out in a torrent, leaving the detritus of unpayable debt and economic catastrophe behind.

After the first attempts at economic rescue in 2009 failed to produce a sustained economic recovery, the confidence of the people diminished. Each new failure by government to deliver the promised return to credit-financed economic growth—the bank bailouts, the make-work spending programs, the reassurances by public officials—eroded the people's confidence, not only in their country but in themselves.

By mid-2009 no one called the economic malaise just a "recession" anymore. The talk first had turned to full-blown economic depression, as unemployment reached 10 percent, and by late 2009 the catastrophe had earned the popular moniker the "Great Recession."

The world's financial leaders, the heads of central banks, the fund managers, the heads of stock exchanges stood stunned, like nuclear scientists after reactor number four blew up at the Chernobyl nuclear power plant in the Soviet socialist republic of Ukraine in 1986. At first they couldn't believe what they were seeing. It wasn't supposed to be possible. All of the safeguards had failed. Later, the scale of the disaster finally sank in.

The first worldwide economic collapse in seventy years encased the globe in a pall of bewilderment and discontent. While Asian and European countries recovered quickly, at least temporarily, in response to government spending programs, in the United States unemployment remained stubbornly high, and the unemployed stayed that way longer than they had during any economic recovery since the Great Depression. Where did all of the prosperity suddenly go? How could this have happened? What will become of us? What shall we do? Will the economy ever recover?

The answer is, Yes, we will get out of this mess. In fact, we have already begun to, but slowly. We will not leap out of this hole we dug for thirty years in a single bound but climb out step by step, ascend not by one dramatic act but by block and tackle, pulling ourselves out by stages as we correct one policy error after another.

The rational approach is to ask, What economic activities are we truly good at as a nation, ones that make us unique and competitive and a constructive player in the new world? How can we do more of these? Also, What are we doing wrong, activities that are not "us," and how can we do fewer of them? The more pressing question is, What kind of economy do we want to have when we emerge? A new version of the credit-based one that just collapsed, built on debt and finance, one that's waiting to implode again after the flow of borrowed government money dries up? That's the course we're on right now.

Unequivocally, if we continue on our current path, we will re-create a version of the economy that just failed, except it will be one with new potential for mayhem in the future, that of a government debt crisis instead of the private debt crisis we had in 2008 and 2009.

We do have options. And that's what *The Postcatastrophe Economy* is about: options. It may sound like a new, productive economy is a pipe dream, especially in the current economic and political climate. The Obama administration, despite early hopes, seems focused on perpetuating the policies of previous presidents by remaining beholden to the finance, insurance, and real estate industries that sank us. And the public seems weary: Why aim for something new when all of us, at all levels—personally, nationally, globally—are desperately seeking a return to the "normal" and familiar, are clinging to any semblance of financial stability by the skin of our teeth? At some level we are all complicit. Who wants the price of their home to fall by 50 percent from artificially inflated levels? And why hope for something new and self-sustaining when government spending saved us from a worse catastrophe, like the one that occurred in the 1930s' debt deflation crisis, and appears to have brought our old economic structure back to life, if only partway?

The bright side of the crisis we're currently facing is that it could serve as a political forcing function for the United States to develop its competitive muscle and eliminate its dependence on foreign borrowing and oil—the main source of our current problems. To execute a true restructuring plan requires strong and uncompromising leaders who are willing to level with the American people, to explain the seriousness of our problems, the sacrifices we all must make to solve them, the new and better nation for ourselves and our children that we will enjoy if we do, and the disaster that awaits us if we fail to meet this challenge.

That sounds good, but how? I argue that we can nurture the seeds of a new American industrial economy—a productive economy that generates profits from technological industries such as computers, biology, medicine, and high-technology materials—by cultivating next-generation transportation, energy, and communications infrastructure. In this book we call it the TECI Economy.

The U.S. economy can reindustrialize around three high-level goals. Within ten years, this country:

- will be the most energy-efficient and least energy-dependent nation in the world;
- will engage the full power of American innovation to develop transportation, energy, and communications infrastructure (TECI) as a

platform for private enterprise to enhance long-term U.S. competitiveness, not an expensive one-off New Deal–style program that promises short-term jobs growth at the price of even higher levels of government debt;

- will maintain merit but remove cost as a barrier to entry to quality education for all members of society, so that Americans have the know-how they need to compete for high-skill, high-wage jobs on a global stage.

These are the fundamentals of the TECI Economy.

To understand how we're going to get to TECI, we need a firm understanding of the economy that just collapsed around us, the one we've been living with for the past thirty years or so—the FIRE (finance, insurance, and real estate) Economy. Many observers regard FIRE as simply the ultimate phase of capitalism. Karl Marx is the most famous among them. He referred to our economic structure as "finance capitalism." Because FIRE has been the underlying basis of the economy since 1980 or so, many adults have known no other. Their work lives have been spent earning a modest income teaching, writing software, driving a truck, managing a store, or any of ten thousand jobs that make up the productive economy, while the big money went to experts in finance. Even professionals in the rarefied income strata of the high-technology and biotech industries could not hope to earn at a level that approached that of the masters of finance on Wall Street. An economy built on making stuff seems old-fashioned at best. The good news is that the United States still makes a lot of stuff, and exports it as well. By developing the productive parts of our economy, and diminishing the nonproductive FIRE sectors, we can grow as a newly competitive economic force in the world.

The FIRE Economy, which was based on financial engineering, capital gains from inflated asset prices, and other nonproductive financial schemes and tended for decades by special interests, grew to great heights and shaded a once vibrant economy below, an economy based on production, saving, and investment. The FIRE Economy also depended on a steady stream of cheap credit and oil, for without it credit-financed consumer spending cannot rise; purchasing power would be sapped by household expenditures on heating fuel and gasoline, and by borrowing at high rates of interest. The solution was to inflate the purchasing power of the U.S. dollar, the currency used for oil trade by the United States and its trade partners, depreciating the price of oil in the process, and to tap into our trade partners' so-called excess savings.

The FIRE Economy is an umbrella term that incorporates the whole dysfunction of the American political economy that has resulted in FIRE industries capturing our government. The same dysfunctional system also produced, among others:

- the military-industrial complex that heavily influences foreign policy;
- the credit-industrial complex that layers economic rents, such as interest payments and fees, on every economic activity, from education to health care, and punishes savers with taxes and rewards debtors with tax deductions;
- the agricultural-industrial complex that has made healthy food expensive and injurious food plentiful and cheap;
- the education-industrial complex that has replaced a competition to produce the best educated students with a contest over who can spend the most money on teachers, school buildings, and technology;
- the health care–industrial complex that profits from illness rather than from preventing it, and adds 40 percent to the costs of medical care without adding value;
- the media-industrial complex that traps the most capable editors and journalists in the role of selling products produced by the FIRE Economy, such as houses during the housing bubble; and
- the prison-industrial complex that creates incentives to incarcerate rather than rehabilitate and prevent criminality.

Most of our so-called economy is dominated by these private enterprises that receive government subsidies through the influence of special interests via lobbies and political action committees. Each of these special interest's self-reinforcing systems, which influence economic policy, must be dismantled, one by one, if the U.S. economy is to recover to reach and surpass its globally competitive position.

The solutions are campaign finance reform and closing the revolving door that operates between private and public institutions.

In the end, the problems that this book describes all come down to the result of thirty years of influence peddling and the capture of our government by special interests, especially by the finance, insurance, and real estate industries. Sales of their main products result in debt that produces a steady stream of revenue from interest payments and fees for themselves but saps the income of every productive business and hardworking wage earner, hospital patient, and student in the United States. An economy dominated by FIRE collapsed, nearly taking the productive economy with it. Yet the seeds of our economic recovery survive, and it is these that we must nurture to grow our economy back. Finance will return as well—to a constructive role in support of the productive economy rather than as the dominant generator of jobs and money in the economy.

So the question arises: How did this FIRE Economy develop?

TALE OF TWO ECONOMIES

The rise of the FIRE Economy is really the story of how certain industries grew from just another sector in the productive economy to our main source of economic growth. Textbooks describe an "economy" as a system made up of producers that employ consumers as workers to manufacture goods and deliver services, in turn paying them wages and salaries that they then spend on goods and services. The consumers' insatiable want of goods and services, combined with their ability to pay for them with cash or credit, is the definition of the term "demand" in economics. Continuous and ever-increasing spending by consumers, and their confidence in their future prospects (consumer confidence), moves the whole economy forward. In this popular but fallacious model, what matters in the economy is that the wage earner consumes. Consumption is the end, not the beginning, of the economic cycle, and saving is a relatively unimportant by-product when a wage earner consumes less than he or she earns.

The productive economy—the economy of goods and services, wages and incomes, employers and employees—grows from profits generated by the sales of goods and services. The profits are earned by firms adding value, like refining or the assembly of inputs such as crude oil or the parts of an automobile.

But since 1980 or so, the U.S. economy has not been just one economy of consumers and producers, but rather two. One economy is of production and consumption driven by the demand of consumers for goods and of producers for profits, much as the textbooks say. That's the productive economy. The other economy is based on finance, what Bill Gross of PIMCO refers to as the "finance-based economy" and Kevin Phillips and Dr. Michael Hudson labeled the Finance, Insurance, and Real Estate, or FIRE, Economy.

The FIRE Economy grows from interest earned on debt and capital gains from the sale of assets, such as real estate, stocks, and bonds. It runs on money lent to the United States from abroad by both private financial institutions and central banks, although since the crisis that began in the early 2000s, more so from the latter. It also runs on money lent into existence within the private credit markets, including mortgages, automobile loans, credit cards, student loans, and health care loans—excessive debt built up from 1980 to 2008 on the assumption that continuous asset price inflation and sufficient economic growth to cover interest expense will continue forever. Those assumptions were wrong.

As we shall see, before it started to collapse in earnest in 2006, the FIRE Economy grew to become much larger than the productive economy. And now, FIRE is in crisis. You see the downside all around us;

the only silver lining is that FIRE may soon return to its place as the cart behind the productive economy horse instead of in front of it.

The FIRE Economy's foundation was debt-based economic growth. Its dominance resulted in deindustrialization and the concentrations of debt, wealth, and income growth in certain sectors of society. The financial sector and U.S. households levered up, borrowing to finance consumption. When the crash came, the government was forced to quickly step in to prevent a catastrophic deleveraging of the financial and household sectors of the economy. Government programs such as the Troubled Asset Relief Fund (TARP) were created to allow financial institutions to unload bad debt. Mortgage refinancing programs were created to help households refinance the mortgages on their homes. In the short run, a repeat of the 1930s crisis was averted, but the consequences of these policies will be felt for decades if they are not addressed.

Unfortunately, the shift from the FIRE Economy to the TECI Economy will not be smooth. We'll travel through a purgatory of high and persistent unemployment, with lower income groups hit the hardest, and high import prices, inflation, stagnant financial markets, civil strife, and a confusion of ad hoc government responses that will as often make matters worse as improve them. This transitional economy is characterized by declining economic output, employment, and household purchasing power. We're living through it right now. There will be bright moments—the Dow Jones Industrial Average breaking 10,000 again in 2009 was taken to be one—but they will be revealed to be an echo of the previous, credit-based boom, unsupported by fundamentals. The economy will not recover with wishful thinking, and governments cannot print either wealth or purchasing power. These must be earned.

Heading into recession with so little fiscal wiggle room, U.S. policy makers had no time or money to waste on a wrong-footed response, yet that is exactly what we got. As we work through this transition to a more productive economy, the limits on government stimulus options grow: Gross external debt is already at 95 percent of GDP; gross public debt, 70 percent of GDP; the U.S. dollar is still at all-time lows even after recent gains; and an effective Fed funds rate a mere 0.5 percent—0 percent for all practical purposes.

Writing stimulus checks to U.S. households in 2008 to pay for one last trip to Home Depot to buy made-in-China goods added $168 billion to our public debt. The $14 billion sent to America's seniors, one $250 check at a time, produced an almost imperceptible blip of economic growth yet left behind a permanent addition to the national debt. Another $700 billion was aimed at bailing out U.S. banks that failed the test of the market. Less widely publicized, the Federal Reserve Bank lent banks $437.5 billion per day in the week ending October 15, 2008, topping the previous week's $420.16 billion per day. These and more than $1 trillion in unmarketable securities of commercial banks a year later remain on the balance sheet of the Federal Reserve. How will the Fed get rid of them? What will happen if they can't? No one knows because this situation has never occurred before.

The financial and financialized companies that our government throws billions at are a dysfunctional part of the U.S. economy. We cannot resuscitate this economy. It's over. The effort to try to bring it back is consuming precious financial resources. Japan made a similar error when it tried to restart its own dysfunctional economy, and for the same reason: lack of political will to repudiate debts built up during Japan's credit bubble era. Japan began in 1993 to reinflate its version of a FIRE Economy when the nation's gross public debt stood at 68 percent of GDP, very close to where the United States was at the beginning of its misguided attempts to move the private debts of homeowners to public account, with government lending and employment programs, starting in 2008. In 2010 Japan's debt approached 200 percent of GDP, twice as high as Jamaica's and nearly as high as Zimbabwe's, yet after decades of fiscal stimuli and 0 percent interest rates its economy is still unable to sustain growth without stimulus; when policy makers attempt to reduce stimulus either by raising interest rates or reduced spending, the economy quickly falls back into recession.

That is where we are headed, except that we are limited to a few years, not the nearly two decades that Japan has pursued this policy. The United States is a foreign debtor that imports capital, not a net creditor like Japan that exports capital. Japan needs only to repay itself. The United States has to repay both its foreign creditors and itself. The United States will run out of foreign credit long before its domestic public debt reaches Japan's astounding level, and will likely run out instead due to the limits of peak cheap oil, as we will see in the chapters ahead. Is it really what we want?

Congress is on the right track with federally funded infrastructure programs that will increase U.S. energy efficiency. Infrastructure development is a valid role for government, to enable private industry to move goods, people, assets, and information more quickly and at lower cost, using less energy per dollar of economic output. However, the form, focus, financing, and fulfillment of these projects are critical to reindustrialization. Private market incentives need to be engaged by government policy, not thwarted by government competition with entrepreneurs and private investors who are working the energy problem and developing novel solutions to remedy the nation's oncoming energy crisis. For example, of $2.4 billion in grants to "Accelerate the Manufacturing and Deployment of the Next Generation of U.S. Batteries and Electric Vehicles" issued as part of the 2009 Recovery Act, $1.5 billion in grants went to "U.S. based manufacturers to produce batteries and their components and to expand battery recycling capacity." Not one of the recipients has produced a single new commercial product. Meanwhile, companies that did not receive government money have to compete with those that did, regardless of the relative merits of the products. Do we want our nation's energy technology companies focused on developing the skills needed to compete with each other for government money, or do we want them to compete to develop the best products for global markets?

Our economy must restructure to remain competitive. It can—if government gets out of the way of technological innovation and assists only where appropriate, where private enterprise cannot operate alone due to excessive risk and capital requirements. Right now, the United

States is embarking on infrastructure programs—the so-called shovel-ready projects that got so much media attention in mid-2009—that will make only marginal improvements to U.S. productivity and competitiveness while vastly expanding the public debt, essentially transferring jobs to the present from the future. Instead, these projects must be chosen carefully, in accordance with one principle—the return on investment. The projects must be financed and managed to minimize costs by imposing the discipline of market competition and at the same time guard against the risk of creating yet another dysfunctional collaboration between private industry and government by special interests, an "infrastructure industrial complex," by requiring free access to all comers. This means public-private partnerships (PPP) that are structured to prevent the kind of wholesale transfer of public assets into the hands of the wealthy and connected, as has occurred in other countries at various times throughout history.

But none of this will matter if we do not immediately and aggressively confront the debt—household debt, corporate debt, public debt, foreign debt—for if left as is the interest payments on these debts will consume too much of the cash flow of families, businesses, and government tax receipts, crippling our ability as a nation to build savings for investment. Make-jobs infrastructure projects that do not improve the ability of the U.S. economy to produce output at lower cost, and do not have the discipline of the private sector to minimize development costs, will lead to decades of economic stagnation by increasing government debt and crowding out private investment. The loss of private investment will, in combination with an exodus of U.S.-trained engineering talent, kill the goose that laid the golden egg: America's risk-taking, creative entrepreneurs and the risk-taking investors who finance their commercial projects.

To finance these projects, public-private partnerships must compete for infrastructure projects to maximize efficiency and minimize costs. To minimize rents, the resulting infrastructure is owned by the public. To minimize fees, tax-free infrastructure bonds are sold—without investment-banking middlemen—by federal and state Treasury departments directly to private and public investors, much as Treasury bonds are sold today via TreasuryDirect.

Foreign governments can purchase minority interests in these firms and projects, providing a safety valve for foreign investors who may otherwise decide not to reinvest in the United States as their Treasury bond holdings mature. Allow U.S. citizens to defer some portion of their taxes to invest in these projects. Structure the bonds to convert to equity once the projects become profitable, to create an incentive for public-private partnerships to design efficiency into the projects from the start to limit taxpayers' potential future liability. Require independently audited reporting and review of milestones during project development.

These core projects will create demand for thousands of satellite start-ups, funded by venture capital and other private equity sources, as well as by government start-up financing programs such as the Small Business Administration (SBA).

Seed-stage financing plants the seeds of early stage technology companies that grow up to be the Apples and Intels of the future. Certain kinds of companies do just fine without this kind of funding and can grow organically from the profits generated by early customers. Dell, for example, grew from the tiny stream of revenue generated by Michael Dell's early customers. But Dell is essentially a computer reseller, not a technology company. Technology companies require hundreds of thousands or even hundreds of millions of dollars at the beginning to bring new inventions to market. One of the most unfortunate results of the collapse of two asset bubbles in ten years is that many so-called angel investors—those who are seed-stage investors in start-up companies—lost their investments not once but twice in a short period of time. They lost money when companies they funded went out of business in the economic downturn of 2001 through 2003, then again in the one that began in late 2007. Even if the companies they financed did not go out of business but were rescued by venture capital firms that supplied fresh cash, the terms of these later financings usually reduced the equity interest of the original seed-stage investors to next to nothing, effectively wiping them out just as if the companies had failed. The venture capitalists are not stepping in to fill the gap because their firms, typically consisting of a half dozen experienced managing partners who actively participate in the companies they invest in, don't have enough manpower to look after more than six to eight companies each. Besides, in the tough financing environment for technology companies, venture capitalists can pay lower, early stage prices for later stage companies and skip all of the risk and development work that an early stage company presents. As a result, very few seeds for tomorrow's technology leaders are getting planted. New private financing initiatives, such as new angel investment groups, will be needed to compensate for the loss of seed-stage financing for technology- and capital-intensive start-ups to develop technologies needed to maximize the economic and social value of the resulting infrastructure.

Using this approach, the United States can avoid wasteful spending and the economically dangerous trend toward socialization of private markets, such as the U.S. housing market, which is currently 90 percent supported by fully nationalized Government Sponsored Enterprises (GSE) Fannie Mae and Freddie Mac. The public policy response to the damage caused by subpar performance of private credit markets following the 2008 credit and banking crisis was socialization of the formerly private housing markets. Prolonged budget deficits that inevitably result from shortfalls in tax revenue during severe recessions followed by slow growth leaves cities and towns without money to pay for infrastructure upkeep and improvements. This will drive a widespread trend toward privatization of public property, such as bridges and roads, over the coming years.

If by the end of 2010 the federal government continues ad hoc public spending programs to create jobs, the United States will find itself deeper in debt, less able to repay it, and no more competitive on the world stage than before, in fact likely less so.

The legacy of the FIRE Economy is a set of economic forces that will heat up the American electorate and produce dramatic political forces for policy change. The four sources of heat are: high unemployment, unpayable debt, inflation in energy and commodity prices due to both currency depreciation and rising oil import prices, and a generation's wealth lost in stock and housing markets that will continue to decline in real (inflation-adjusted) terms for another decade or more. Even after losing more than 10 percent in nominal (not inflation-adjusted) terms in the decade since the year 2000, the decade ahead may be even less hospitable to equity investors if our current direction is maintained.

Much as the great inflation crisis of the late 1970s gave the U.S. leadership the political will to make painful adjustments to economic and monetary policy, a grinding deterioration in living standards will drive American policy makers to return to the core values that made the country vital: an unparalleled capacity for innovation, a spirit of fair competition, a strong work ethic, a willingness to take risks, a tolerance for failure, a culture of self-reliance, a willingness to forgo immediate gratification by saving for the future, a desire to pull one's own weight, and a respect for the rights of others.

We must not let the opportunity slip past us. The Obama administration could have used the financial and economic crisis as a forcing function for real change, but the Obama administration is not using our nation's remaining foreign and domestic government credit to build a solid foundation for capital formation and to make our economy more competitive by improving energy infrastructure and bolstering productive enterprise. Instead it has continued the FIRE Economy–friendly policies of previous administrations, both Democratic and Republican, in a desperate bid to restart it. Financial sector interests have maintained their influence over the political process.

The bailouts of AIG and GM, the "Cash for Clunkers" program, refinancings of mortgages on homes that borrowers could not afford in the first place, the Fed's purchases of asset-backed securities, and other crisis policies make the administration's political orientation clear: Rather than find ways to restructure the bad debt left behind by thirty years of the FIRE Economy, the Federal Reserve and Treasury

Department are moving the bad private debts on the accounts of commercial banks onto the public accounts of the Treasury Department and Federal Reserve. They are shifting the credit risk that caused the private credit markets to collapse onto the public sector, leaving the United States vulnerable to a government debt crisis in the process.

FIRE Economy interests still have Washington locked up tight. Banking and finance reforms have been sidelined or watered down. Obama's health care reforms revealed how effectively the insurance industry can shape public debate, as a critical public discussion about how to effectively and economically provide health care devolved quickly into a fistfight over "death panels" and socialism. Financial institutions begged for public money in 2008 with the threat of economic collapse if they didn't get it. A year later the employees of these same firms earned obscene bonuses funded by emergency public loans and bailouts.

Heading into an active election period from 2010 to 2012, the scent if not the stench of third world–style corruption hangs in the air. Politicians who make the mistake that the American public has a poor sense of smell, and who fail to acknowledge the special interests' influence that have perverted the U.S. economy, will find themselves voted out, no matter their party affiliation. Voters are connecting the dots. They will demand accountability and a restoration of government for all of the people, not only for those with money, power, and influence.

For all of the troubles and crises that the FIRE Economy has visited upon the American people, it will not go quietly into the night. Let this book serve as a warning to Americans of the dangers that lay ahead if we do not change course, and also a vision of a promising future if only we can.

THE KNOW-HOW EXISTS

During the rise of the FIRE Economy, the Productive Economy never went away; it morphed and improved. It figured out how to work within and accommodate the FIRE system, and to a certain extent even embraced it, such as during the technology stock bubble of the late 1990s. While the absurdly high returns offered by trading inflated assets—buildings, stocks, bonds—back and forth attracted the best and the brightest with absurd salaries and capital gains, the productive economy figured out not only how to survive but how to thrive under the umbrella. Entrepreneurs did as they always have: They adapted.

Engineers and scientists, driven by the desire to solve problems (and get rich doing it), toil to invent new products and services to solve their customers' problems. Entrepreneurs build new businesses around those great inventions that solve a problem that has never been solved that way before. Sometimes the person who understands the customer's problem and the solution—the entrepreneur and the inventor—are the same person. In this book we refer to these technically adept entrepreneurs, who are at times inventing entirely new industries and taking the economy forward in new directions, as "inventive entrepreneurs" to distinguish them from business leaders who may build new companies in existing industries but are not breaking new technical ground.

Collectively, over time, inventive entrepreneurs create the apparent free lunch of economic growth of rising productivity and living standards: safer and more reliable cars, miraculous medical advances, cleaner burning fuels, and computer networks that let us work and communicate from home. In the future new inventions will produce advances, such as, in the field of biotechnology, microorganisms that can turn nuclear waste into harmless by-products and, in nanotechnology, paints that dynamically reflect heat but not light, reducing the amount of energy needed to heat and cool buildings.

Entrepreneurs create wealth apparently out of thin air in a deceptively simple fashion—at least it's easy to describe, although it's much harder to do than it sounds. All entrepreneurs who create new companies operate on the principle that if you solve one customer's problem in a new and unique way, often using a new technology or business model, at a cost that is less than the price that the product or service can be sold for, and if you can economically reach a large and growing market of other customers like them, then four things happen. One, thousands or millions of people who had a problem no longer do. Two, people who were previously unemployed are hired and earn an income they can save, spend, and reinvest. Three, the founders make money that they will save, spend, and reinvest. Four, investors will make money—real money, based on profits from solving a customer problem and not from inflating an asset price—that they can save, spend, and reinvest.

The heart of the system of productive, entrepreneurial economic growth is the idea that in America you can get rich solving other people's problems with a minimum of interference by government. By their nature, inventive entrepreneurs are problem solvers, just as explorers are in their hearts adventurers. They may found, or work in, start-up companies, but many entrepreneurs exist within large companies where they battle bureaucracy and internal politics on a mission to get their innovative products and services ideas to market. Here is the secret of America's success: a culture and economy that encourages and nurtures an army of problem solvers.

Society benefits indirectly from inventive entrepreneurs through the benefits of higher productivity and living standards for all. But most nations try to exploit inventive entrepreneurs' creativity and willingness to take risks by imposing taxes and fees at the very earliest stages of the development of their companies, such as payroll taxes, health insurance, and a minimum wage that large companies can afford to pay. This creates barriers to entrepreneurial activity. Entrepreneur-friendly countries are dynamic, fast growing, and technologically advanced, while countries that discourage entrepreneurs with taxation, bureaucracy, and weak intellectual property rights enforcement, and fail to provide an adequate regulatory environment, stagnate and decline as entrepreneurs leave to go to countries where they can do what they do: solve problems and, yes, get rich doing it.

China, for example, has a strong entrepreneurial culture but weak institutions for financing innovation and no recent history of intellectual property rights protection. No surprise that few technological innovations have been invented in China that have been widely adopted outside the country. Why bother to go to the trouble to invent when the fruits of your labor can be copied and sold with impunity?

The cost of starting a company in most European countries is prohibitive. Not only are the legal costs of incorporation high, often thousands or even tens of thousands of dollars, but entrepreneurs face high taxes on their payroll, just like large companies.

Since the founding of the republic, America has been the place that the world's most creative and inventive minds have come to because it has been the place where the entire ecosystem of education, financing, smart regulation, and financial markets exist all together to allow inventive entrepreneurs to fulfill their dreams. The U.S. system of technical entrepreneurship is a functional whole, a virtuous chain of talent, passion, and money.

The United States may not have the most engineers, but it has the best trained and the most creative. India produces 350,000 engineers per year to America's 75,000, but Microsoft, Google, and Intel are American companies. However, the rest of world has caught on to the value of the national economic resource that inventive entrepreneurs represent, while the United States appears to have forgotten it.

That's the greatest threat to this productive economy: The fallout from the demise of the FIRE Economy, in the form of protectionism, taxation, and support for finance and big business, will dampen the spirit of inventive entrepreneurship by breaking the virtuous chain that allowed companies from Intel to Google to develop in the United States. We can't let that happen.

For instance, every year, the United States sends home thousands of foreign-born engineers due to immigration laws that in 2008 limited a special visa for engineers, called H-1B, to 65,000. (The H-1B is a nonimmigrant visa that allows U.S. employers to employ foreign guest workers in specialty occupations.) For decades engineers, physicists, and other technically trained professionals received the world's most advanced education at Stanford, MIT, and other great American universities. This army of foreign-born, U.S.-trained technologists used to remain in the United States for the unique opportunity to start new companies that not only created millions of jobs but advanced the U.S. economy through improved productivity and products for export. Now many return home because either opportunities to build businesses are better there or U.S. immigration laws send them home. The United States is training and then exporting not only a critical engine of its growth, but of its recovery.

Meanwhile, as the Great Recession dragged on, large companies such as automakers, which employ thousands of workers and represent huge blocks of voters, vied with banks and other financial institutions for public funds, none of which were raised via taxation but all by additional government borrowing. The total amount of debt that a country can support is limited. If public debt levels rise, private debt levels must fall such that the total level of both private and public debt combined stays below a certain threshold. Otherwise, bad things happen, such as rising interest rates. So, increasing debt in the public sector to protect big companies means less private credit is available to small businesses that always bring the U.S. economy out of recession by creating new jobs, income, and savings.

While the federal government has never invented anything, it does have a role to play. In the past it has funded very large technical projects that engaged inventors and entrepreneurs and paved the road to much larger developments in the future. The Manhattan Project and the Internet are two obvious examples. Here the government does have a constructive role to play in encouraging the nation's army of problem solvers, its entrepreneurs, in two ways. First, it can support the commercialization of technologies already under development, and second, it can launch new commercially viable projects.

Even in the best of times, entrepreneurs and inventors confront the compound risks of business failure on a daily basis: lack of funds, product failures, and competition, to name three. The additional burdens of taxes and insurance can often make the difference between success and failure. If those burdens are high enough, and private financing becomes both scarce and expensive because liquidity in the initial public offering (IPO) and merger-and-acquisition (M&A) markets for high-tech companies remains well below historical norms, entrepreneurs will become discouraged from even trying to start new companies in the United States. They will move to countries where the overall start-up growth environment is more favorable.

To drive the transformation of the TECI Economy in the long run, we will need many more inventive entrepreneurs. That's why programs in U.S. high schools and universities must be devoted to educating a whole new generation of inventive entrepreneurs.

The heroes of the FIRE Economy were the financial engineers and alchemists who turned arcane mathematical theory into gold for financial firms determined to make a quick buck. The heroes of the TECI Economy will be the mechanical, biological, structural, electrical, and civil engineers who build wealth the sure, slow way, by gradual improvement of the physical world around them, and through saving and investment.

WHO I AM

My background is as an entrepreneur who has built and raised $30 million in venture capital to finance start-up technology companies after spending more than twenty years in the high technology industry in various operating roles, from writing software to managing products to executive sales and marketing roles to the CEO of venture capital–backed companies. I also spent several years on the other side of the table, working for an early stage technology company venture capital firm, Osborn Capital, and later for a large $1.6 billion later stage venture capital firm, Trident Capital. As a macroeconomic analyst, I spend most of my time studying and crunching numbers issued by dozens of government and nongovernment organizations both here and abroad, from the U.S. Department of Commerce to the Organization for Economic Co-operation and Development (OECD). I also read dozens of the major finance and economics news sources, from the *Wall Street Journal* to the *Financial Times* to the *Asia Times*, to see what others are saying, or not saying, about the latest events in the world of finance and economics. I start my investigations by looking at the latest data for anomalies and unexpected changes. The data leads to questions, and the questions take the analysis forward.

For example, reading over the Treasury Department data in the summer of 2009, I wondered how the United States could continue its current astounding and rapidly increasing rate of debt issuance when so little of this debt was being purchased by foreign investors.

The Treasury issued over $557 billion in mostly short-term debt in August 2009 alone, out of $2 trillion issued over the past year—28 percent of the annual issuance in one month. Yet the total year over year net increase in foreign holdings was only $250 billion. That means domestic purchasers were buying nearly 90 percent of all the debt we issue. Who in the United States was buying all of this newly issued debt? According to the December 2009 quarterly report of the Federal Reserve, called the "Flow of Funds," of the $1.8 trillion worth of Treasury bonds bought by domestic purchasers, $550 billion were bought by U.S. households, and the remaining $1.25 trillion was purchased by U.S. financial institutions, such as commercial banks. This is how the United States has financed its spending programs since late 2008.

Can this level of domestic borrowing continue? What happens if it does not? How long will our foreign creditors tolerate this? What happens if they stop tolerating it? They can legitimately worry that when push comes to shove, domestic lenders are more likely to be first in line ahead of foreign lenders if the United States should get into trouble repaying its debt.

The data tell me what is happening now, but not what is likely to happen in the future. For that I need a process framework. All change is driven by process. My theory, going back to more than a decade of experience as a product manager in the high-tech industry, is that if you can understand the underlying process—the primary elements and dynamics of change in the economy—you can forecast how the economy will tend to change over time.

For example, when I was raising venture capital as CEO of wireless security company Bluesocket in 2001, I created a diagram that forecast the development of the wireless LAN security market. The model's purpose was to help me make decisions about things such as hiring new employees or timing an exit when the company was likely to have the greatest value in the mergers and acquisitions market.

It turned out to be more or less correct.

I performed a similar analysis for my company iTulip.com, which was first launched in November 1998, when the stock market bubble was fully inflated. My company was one of the first and very few to warn visitors not to put their retirement money in the speculative bubble that the U.S. stock markets had become. At the time, Jim Cramer was ranting on CNBC about the latest dot-com "can't lose" stock. We warned that the stock market was due to crash, most likely by the first or second quarter of 2000. It did.

In August 2002, the stock market was in the toilet, as iTulip had forecast in 1999. We had just gone through a short recession, and the Fed and Congress were furiously pumping the system up, cutting rates and slashing taxes as I had forecast in 2001 when I made a decision to make a major investment in gold despite the ideological and near religious baggage attached to it. At the time the price was $265 after falling in price for over twenty years. I made my argument in an August 2001 article published on iTulip.com titled "Questioning Popular Financial Advice." Gold was nearly universally considered about the worst investment you could make, and if you bought it in 1980 indeed it had been. But I thought it looked cheap, and with an indeterminably long period of fiscal and monetary mismanagement that lay ahead, the price had only one direction to go—up. Not only has it gone up since 2001, but the gold price has not ended below the starting price since. Gold has outpaced the S&P and DOW by a wide margin, rising over 300 percent while stocks, including dividends, are up less than 20 percent nominally and off more than 10 percent in inflation-adjusted terms. The gold price went up for nearly ten years with little volatility compared to stock prices, the exact opposite of what gold is generally expected to do.

I received many letters of thanks from visitors who had gotten out of the stock market in time with their retirement accounts intact. Mission accomplished, iTulip.com went off the air, and I went off to run Bluesocket at the request of the board.

Fast-forward to March 2006. The NASDAQ had mostly stayed in the dumper, with various dot-com stinkers sinking and disappearing into the history books, again, predictably. The Dow Jones Industrial Average, through a combination of a reconstituting of the easily manipulated thirty-stock index—throwing out some losers and adding in some winners—and inflation had fought its way back to where it had been six years earlier—flat. Except that, adjusted for inflation, it was down about 20 percent. But that didn't keep Cramer from returning to CNBC to rant and throw chairs around while touting the latest can't lose stocks. What really kept the United States out of the poorhouse was the housing bubble. I failed to predict the housing bubble in 2001 as the Fed's answer to the stock market bubble collapse; in fact, I argued that the Fed would *never* allow one to develop.

I was wrong.

My thinking was that, in the past, the Fed had traditionally been very quick to stop speculation in real estate, much more quickly than it did stock market speculation. Why? Real estate involves the banking system much more than the stock market does, and looking after the banking system is job one for the Fed. Letting millions of homeowners buy real estate they can't afford with mortgages they can never pay back is a surefire road to mass defaults that can cripple the banking system. When a relatively normal housing cycle boom ended in the early 1990s, the U.S. banking system seized up. That response to the downside of that minor real estate cycle was a petit mal seizure compared to the massive stroke that the banking system suffered after the real estate freak show that ran from 2002 to 2006.

The Federal Reserve and other bank regulators had every motive to prevent a housing bubble from developing. The political aftermath of a real estate bubble historically in every nation where they have occurred is macroeconomic devastation of the host country's economy and a banking crisis. The inevitable outcome is economic recession and high unemployment, falling incomes, contracting credit, and negative wealth effects. These combine to keep consumers home sulking and saving, not out at the mall buying goods. This presented a risk unique to the United States, because the money to purchase the goods was largely borrowed from the goods-exporting countries themselves— Asia for consumer electronics and the Middle East for oil. That demand motivates Asian and Middle Eastern countries to lend to the United States. The vicious circle of lending, borrowing, and importing starts with the U.S. consumer. A crashed housing bubble is certain to disrupt this arrangement. I had no reason to think that the Fed and other regulators, acting rationally, would ever put the long-term economic balance between the United States and its trade partners at risk with the politically short-term expedient of a housing bubble.

If I'd been listening more carefully, I would have heard Fed chairman Alan Greenspan noting in public hearings in 1999, when one senator wondered aloud if Greenspan was worried about the inevitable collapse of the stock market bubble, that only a small percentage of U.S. households own stocks, whereas 70 percent of household wealth is tied up in real estate. Don't worry about it. We've got a plan.

Alas, I missed the cue in the early days and did not catch up until August 2002, when I identified the housing market as the start of a bubble that was likely to last for several years. It was a reminder of how important it is to fully understand the underlying political and economic processes involved. None of us can afford to miss events of the scale of housing bubbles. The fact that financial and banking system regulators had been captured by the interests of the financial industry and big business came as a revelation years later, in 2006, but in retrospect, it should have been obvious. Getting it right is imperative if we, as investors, homeowners, parents, and workers, are to navigate the complicated world of the political economy so that we can all enjoy a more secure financial future, protected from the busts that appear to be a recurring feature of our system. Careful analysis is also critical for all of us to understand how the FIRE Economy developed, grew, and burned, and how we can get out of our current mess. It won't be easy—a question simply of picking the right stocks or shoveling bailout money at short-lived projects like bridge repairs—but worthwhile things rarely are.

The only way to produce purchasing power is by the creation of wealth, and the only way to create wealth is through saving and innovation. In spite of all of the bad news readers will confront in this book, I never lose sight of America's core competencies, the things that will allow the United States to prevail in the future: its size; its culture of risk taking and invention; its sense of fairness; its respect for its people's rights and freedoms regardless of class, race, or ethnicity; its respect for the rule of law; and its penchant for pragmatism. The reindustrialized TECI Economy will thrive in an environment of minimal special interest interference and extraction of economic rents.

Before we can understand where we are going—how the TECI Economy can develop and what it might eventually look like—and before we can find our way through the transitional economy, we must first understand how we got here and where we came from—the origins of the FIRE Economy. After we cover those basics, as well as how it grew, we'll turn to TECI itself, and then finish with two chapters of more detailed macroeconomic and financial analysis about what the next decade is likely to look like as we work to cure our massive debt hangover.

PART I

—

THE FIRE ECONOMY

CHAPTER 1

—

THE FOUNDATIONS OF THE FIRE
ECONOMY—AND HOW THEY CRUMBLED

OWE, v. To have (and to hold) a debt. The word formerly signified not indebtedness, but possession; it meant "own," and in the minds of debtors there is still a good deal of confusion between assets and liabilities.

—AMBROSE BIERCE (1842–1914),
THE DEVIL'S DICTIONARY

After World War II the United States turned its wartime military-industrial might to rebuilding its own civilian economy and the economies abroad that had been devastated by war. To keep a sudden withdrawal of wartime spending and production from pushing the U.S. economy into recession—as had happened after the end of World War I—America started on infrastructure development that had been delayed by years of war spending and a lack of manpower. A new national highway system and a scaled-up housing industry softened the blow to the economy as wartime industry was scaled back. In the decade after the war the U.S. economy was transitioned from the world's greatest war machine to its most productive civilian economy, confounding the predictions of economists that without the economic

—

stimulus of war, the U.S. economy was destined to collapse back into a new great depression.

In the twenty-five years after World War II the U.S. economy expanded more than fourfold, from $223 billion in Gross National Product (GNP) in 1946 to just over $1 trillion in 1970, while the rest of the industrial world purchased U.S. exports as part of reconstruction. Capitalist industrial nations in Europe and Asia recovered from the war with astonishing speed, and by the early 1970s the United States faced global competition again for the first time since the 1920s. In the late 1960s, for the first time in its history, the United States ran into trouble financing its trade with the rest of the world.

The FIRE Economy was America's answer to this rising foreign competition. Its pillars, which we discussed briefly in the introduction, include the dollar cartel, financialization, the fat spread, credit risk pollution, and regulatory capture. And, lest we forget how the FIRE Economy was marketed, we have to consider the role of certain business media outlets in propagating the ten fallacies of the FIRE Economy.

THE DOLLAR CARTEL

In the first few months of 1971, America developed its first ever "current account" deficit; that is, it owed its trade partners more on the value of imports than it earned in exports. In the first quarter of that year the United States ran a trade deficit of $400 million. To such a large economy that deficit looks small by today's standards, a mere 0.1 percent of GDP. But that was enough to send U.S. trade partners scrambling for repayment in U.S. Treasury gold rather than paper dollars, as they feared the dollar either had been or was about to be devalued, cutting the purchasing power of the dollars they were owed.

Under the Bretton Woods monetary system that was hammered out in 1944 in the closing months of the war, nations had a choice of payment for international transactions in either local currency or gold. The system was designed to keep countries honest, to thwart the overpowering desire of governments to devalue a national currency to make exports less expensive on the global market, and thus more competitive—a tendency that becomes irresistible in such times of global contraction and deflation as occurred in the 1930s, to the great detriment of global trade. (We'll touch on this important dynamic later in the book, because it is highly relevant to our current plight.) In 1971, the U.S. trade deficit led its trade partners to fear that the United States either had or planned to devalue the dollar to protect American interests.

The United States did not have enough gold to pay all of the foreign claims and did not want to take the necessary but politically inexpedient steps—such as raising short-term U.S. interest rates—to restructure the economy, improving competitiveness as a producer and saver by pursuing policies designed to expand the nation's exports and increase savings in the long run but sure to push an already weakened U.S. economy into recession in the short term. Instead, President Nixon "temporarily" suspended gold convertibility of the dollar while promising not to devalue the dollar.

Gold convertibility was never restored. In effect, the United States unilaterally abrogated the Bretton Woods monetary system. Two years later, in 1973, Nixon devalued the dollar not once, but twice.

A decade of international currency chaos followed, culminating in double-digit inflation in the United States and in many countries around the world. Out of that chaos arose the first pillar of the FIRE Economy: the dollar cartel. The international arrangement evolved to allow the United States to back its currency not with gold but with U.S. Treasury bonds. In effect, it meant that the world had to trust the United States to manage inflation with great discipline—to maintain the purchasing power of the dollar and make it as good as if the currency were backed by gold.

Any country that trades with the United States has to purchase dollars on the foreign exchange market to convert the local currency— yen, pesos, rubles—to dollars to settle the transaction. The Federal Reserve, under the leadership of Arthur Burns from 1970 to 1978, quickly became alarmed at the size of the money supply building up outside the United States, beyond the control of U.S. authorities. In response, the Fed developed a program to allow currency reserves to be held on foreign account at the Fed in the form of U.S. Treasury bonds earning interest. This expedient later grew into an enormous stock of Treasury debt that appears as an added debt liability of the United States to its trade partners.

Another consequence of the arrangement was that many transactions worldwide continued to be conducted in dollars, even those not conducted directly with the United States. When Japan, for example, purchases oil from Saudi Arabia, the Japanese importer has to purchase dollars on the foreign exchange market to execute the transaction. The demand for dollars in these transactions, amounting to net positive demand for millions or billions of dollars per day, as well as the net accumulation of dollar-denominated assets from trade with the United States, created a dollar demand that no other nation's currency enjoyed.

Every other nation except the United States has to earn a strong currency through a positive balance of trade and sound fiscal and monetary policy. For any other country with as large a net foreign debt position as the United States, even a whiff of inflation in the floating exchange rate system sends the currency tumbling, as foreign investors flee, fearing the loss of purchasing power of their holdings. The dollar, however, is unique: Demand for dollars that is in no way connected to the U.S. economy or its monetary or fiscal policy means that the exchange rate value of the dollar is artificially inflated. This is the dollar cartel.

Why does the artificial demand for dollars created by the dollar cartel matter? The price of a good, according to standard economic theory, is determined by the supply of that good and demand for it, but that is only half the story. Prices are also affected by the supply of and demand for the currency in which the good is priced. If you hold the supply and demand for a good steady but increase the supply of dollars in the economy, the price of that good goes down. If, however, the demand for a currency is greater than the supply, then prices of items in that currency fall.

The flipside of currency with a value inflated by artificial demand is depreciation in the price of goods purchased with that currency. As a consequence of the dollar cartel, the United States has for over thirty years been able to purchase the exports of other countries, such as oil from the Middle East, at a discount. Other countries that purchase oil in dollars benefit from the arrangement, too—thus the term dollar cartel. Artificially cheap oil, deflated in price by overpriced dollars, allowed the United States to develop an energy-inefficient transportation infrastructure while at the same time inducing oil producers to use up nonrenewable national resources at a higher rate than might have occurred if market forces determined the purchasing power of the dollar, and thus oil prices. In other words, the United States, Europe, and Asia got oil producers to use up their best oil rapidly, at bargain prices, accelerating the run-up to the condition that I call peak cheap oil, when there is still plenty of oil but finding and producing it becomes increasingly more difficult and expensive (see chapter 5 for more on this phenomenon).

In self-defense, in the 1970s oil producers ramped up the Organization of the Petroleum Exporting Countries (OPEC), which had originally been formed in the 1960s to attempt to control the supply side of the price equation to maintain prices. OPEC briefly succeeded in raising oil prices with an embargo of oil shipments to the United States in the late 1970s but has been relatively ineffective ever since.

With a built-in demand for dollars that did not depend on export earnings, and with U.S. trade partners accumulating dollars, not only did the dollar strengthen for fundamental reasons, but, in part due to the continuous capital inflows into the United States, interest rates fell. One measure of the growth of the FIRE Economy between the early 1980s and the beginning of the end in 2006 was the U.S. current account deficit. It ballooned by a factor of 158 while the U.S. economy grew by a factor of only 12. The popular explanation for this development is that the world needs a developed country to absorb the output of developing countries, and that the United States, with its status as the world's largest economy, is in the best position to accumulate the debt that is the natural result of this process if it goes on for an extended period. Ironically, today the United States has a more precarious external debt position than the trade partners it supposedly helped through this arrangement. The precondition for the growth of the FIRE Economy that existed in the early 1980s, a relatively strong fiscal and trade deficit position, no longer exists. The FIRE Economy simply cannot continue.

By accident or design, the dollar cartel, the first pillar of the FIRE Economy, guaranteed a steady stream of capital into the United States, regardless of its economy's ability to pay in goods of equal value, something no other country has been able to maintain for so long. By accident, not design, the second pillar of the FIRE Economy, financialization, developed as interest rates on a benchmark ten-year U.S. Treasury bond declined from a historic peak of over 15 percent in 1981 to under 5 percent in 1998.

FINANCIALIZATION

The second pillar of the FIRE Economy is financialization, the incursion of finance into every aspect of American business and economic life, which changed the way consumers buy automobiles and U.S. automakers run their businesses, the way students pay for school and universities fund their operations, the way homes are financed and consumer goods acquired. In short, credit became the biggest American business of all. More than anything else, the FIRE Economy ran on credit, and credit creates debt.

Financialization was a by-product of the period of currency chaos, from 1971 to 1980, that produced great inflation. For the latter half of that decade, inflation in the United States exploded from single to double digits as the cost of the Vietnam War and President Lyndon Johnson's Great Society spending programs stretched the nation's finances, the recession caused goods supply shortages relative to the money supply, and the OPEC oil embargo made energy prices spike.

The politically convenient political orthodoxy of the Nixon and Carter eras is that an acceptable unemployment rate can be maintained without creating inflation. But then Milton Friedman, among others, arrived to show that any attempt to manage an economy at a set rate of unemployment was doomed to produce inflation.

According to the economics orthodoxy adopted by academic and government economists in the era that followed in the early 1980s, wages are the primary mechanism for the transmission of inflation into goods and services prices in an economy, leading to a wage-price spiral. Managing wage inflation came to be regarded as the cornerstone of sound monetary policy. (The Fed's own research contradicts this, as we'll see later.) The wage pricing power of trade unions diminished as double-digit unemployment during the early 1980s recessions virtually eliminated workers' bargaining power. After the 1980s, trade unions ceased to be a relevant mechanism for transmitting rising commodity prices into the economy through negotiated wage increases. Liberalization of immigration policy and outsourcing of U.S. production and services jobs in the 1990s was—along with deregulation of finance and tax cuts—a central tenet of FIRE Economy policy that produced the miracle of low interest rates, low unemployment, and low commodity price inflation, even as asset prices inflated by double digits yearly. Low wage rates were a result of free-market principles promoted by Milton Friedman and his followers in the Reagan administration in the early 1980s. Under the banner of "free markets," these principles replaced the Keynesian interventionist policies seemingly discredited by a combination of inflation and recession—labeled "stagflation"—in the late 1970s and the failed economic policies of Presidents Richard Nixon, Gerald Ford, and Jimmy Carter. Ford's most damning misstep was his administration's ludicrous "Whip Inflation Now" program. WIN buttons got the country exactly nowhere. Inflation cannot be willed away; it can only be controlled by containing the money supply and by making sound policy decisions, in particular budget decisions, that support the exchange rate value of the currency.

These so-called free market policies were only "free" for those industries that benefited the most from low inflation and wage rates. The policies that supported the so-called free market included:

- **low taxes:** sold under rubrics such as "Markets are more efficient than governments at allocating capital" and "Consumers make more rational decisions with their money than governments can." *Intent*: Free up household and business cash flow to increase money available in the economy to pay interest payments on debt to lenders. *Results*: Rapid inflation in the prices of services—such as medical care, education, and housing—financed with credit; indebtedness of households; creation of the two-income household; lack of investment in public goods, such as infrastructure; massive increase in public debt.
- **financial deregulation:** sold as "Creating more efficient markets." *Intent*: asset price inflation to increase profits for finance, insurance, and real estate firms. *Results*: credit risk pollution, the infusion of credit default risk throughout the credit markets, leading to the credit crash of 2007 and the credit crunch thereafter.
- **democratization of credit:** sold as "Giving wage earners access to credit previously only available to high-income earners and corporations." *Intent*: charge high interest rates to high-risk borrowers who also have a record of high repayment rates. *Results*: Reduced the ability of households to pay bills and save money on one income. With 70 percent of U.S. households living one paycheck away from insolvency, overindebtedness reduced their ability to negotiate wage hikes with employers, because the loss of income by either breadwinner for even a few months spelled bankruptcy. Wage rates stagnated even as the prices of goods, and especially of insurance, education, and housing, went up. Thus began the era of the monthly payment consumer, a consumer who

prices goods and services based on monthly payments versus total cash price. An auto purchase was no longer made on the basis of comparing a $20,000 model to one costing $30,000. The question came down to financing, i.e., whether the $20,000 car could be purchased on credit for $500 a month on a forty-eight-month loan or the $30,000 car for seventy-two months for $525 per month. Given the choice, the monthly payment consumer often picked the latter, even though that meant paying $7,700 in interest compared to $3,800.

- **weak enforcement of immigration law:** sold as "openness." *Intent*: increase competition among wage earners and thus suppress wages. *Results*: Increased labor competition limits the wage pricing power of domestic workers, leading to increased reliance on debt to finance household expenditures and the use of debt by local and state governments to finance spending on education and other services previously financed via tax receipts.
- **liberal outsourcing policy:** sold as "Free markets do a better job at allocating wage rates across borders; it helps raise the living standards of people in emerging markets by providing employment and of U.S. citizens by lowering the prices of imported goods." *Intent*: Similar to the effect of the demise of unions on the wages of U.S. workers in the manufacturing industry, outsourcing reduced the pricing power of wage earners in a range of industries, from software development to law. *Results*: a decline in wage relative to the prices of goods and services, reduced living standards, and a decline in the quality of life for the American middle class.

FIRE Economy policies had the net result of lowering taxes for households and businesses so that more household and corporate cash flow was available to be spent on servicing debt owed to creditors. But what caused the financialization of productive industries in the United States?

THE FAT SPREAD

The high inflation of the 1970s hammered Wall Street's financial firms. By 1979 some top firms traded as penny stocks as investors fled paper assets for hard assets like gold, oil, and land. But the great inflation did have one long-lasting benefit: It wiped out much of the consumer and business debt that had built up on balance sheets over the previous twenty years. Wage inflation of 10 percent or more per year allowed existing fixed-interest debt payments to be quickly repaid, while high interest rates discouraged new borrowing. The result was a huge increase in saving. A $400-per-month mortgage could be repaid more quickly from a $20,000 annual income than a $15,000 income. By the time the Federal Reserve attacked inflation in 1980 with breathtaking increases in short-term interest rates, household and corporate balance sheets were largely cleared of debt; the debts had been inflated away. America was debt-free, ready to reload.

And reload it did. The FIRE Economy produced a gigantic credit bubble—just like the one described in the excerpt from the *Quarterly Journal of Economics* that opens this book.

In addition to the dollar cartel and financialization, the FIRE Economy was built on one other effect: the "fat spread" that resulted from the fall of interest rates after 1980.

The Fed under Paul Volcker—the economist appointed by Jimmy Carter in 1979 and reappointed by Ronald Reagan to chair the Federal Reserve, and who served until 1987—raised short-term interest rates to 19 percent, a full 7 percent over the rate of inflation. Shocked investors ran from the hard assets where they had taken refuge from inflation in the 1970s, back into financial assets like stocks and bonds that offered a higher real rate of return, even with inflation at 12 percent. With short-term rates at 19 percent, inflation didn't stay high for long. That radical prescription put the U.S. economy through two major recessions in three years. As unemployment reached double digits, wage earners lost pricing power and union membership declined from an all-time peak of 22 percent in 1975 to a low of 12 percent by 2006.

This is not an endorsement of trade unions but rather an observation of the impact of economic policy on them.

The fat spread is the difference between the high but falling whole-sale borrowing rates paid by banks and the more gradual decline in interest rates—and in many cases no decline, or even a rise—in interest rates paid by retail borrowers. Between 1980 and 1990, rates paid by banks fell from double to single digits, while the rates paid by borrowers fell more slowly, especially for credit card and auto loan borrowers. This made lending more profitable than most forms of production, with the exception of companies whose cost of goods was effectively zero, like those that produced products such as software. No surprise, then, that even manufacturers and retail trade companies wanted in on the lending business, including automobile manufacturers such as General Motors, with GMAC, and Ford Motor, with Ford Motor Credit, and chain stores such as Sears and JCPenney. Previously companies offered layaway plans, which force the customer to save money to buy the product. When the layaway account reached the amount of the purchase price of the product, the customer then received it from the company—without incurring an interest expense. GMAC became the first company to make debt-based financing available to customers on a wide scale. Since Henry Ford personally disliked the concept of his customers going into debt to buy his products, Ford did not offer such plans until decades after GMAC did.

Close inspection of the income statements of many U.S. consumer goods companies reveals that lending money became a vital part of their business as they played the fat spread, compliments of the FIRE Economy. By 2008, GM earned most of its profits from financing and lost money on every car. Insidiously, financialization reduced the competitiveness of U.S. manufacturers; when the FIRE Economy crashed, it left manufacturers like GM unable to make profits in the same way that their overseas competitors could, since the latter did not depend heavily on financing to earn profits but instead profited the old-fashioned way, by selling cars one by one for less than the total cost of design, manufacture, marketing, sales, and distribution.

When the fat spread effect began to run out in the mid-1990s, the FIRE Economy had its first major crisis. In response, bank reserves rules and account regulations were changed to extend the credit boom. Once those benefits ran out in the early 2000s, lower lending standards, low interest rates, and financially engineered debt products enabled by newly deregulated debt markets, together with emergency rate cuts by the Fed in 2001, extended the credit boom for one final spurt of growth that we know today as the housing bubble. This growth also included less widely discussed booms in debt used to finance commercial real estate, leveraged buyouts, M&A activity, and other nonproductive FIRE games. At its height, the U.S. credit machine was producing five dollars of new debt for every dollar of GDP growth, up from a ratio of only one to one in 1980 when the FIRE Economy began.

CREDIT RISK POLLUTION

Since the dawn of the Industrial Age, dilution has been the policy of choice when dealing with the pollutant by-products of manufacturing. Until the 1960s, unregulated industrial companies polluted the ecosystem with toxic waste from manufacturing processes. It worked until the volume and toxicity of the pollutants exceeded the capacity of the ecosystem to absorb them. The most toxic man-made organic chemical is dioxin. The most famous case of dioxin pollution took place around Love Canal in Niagara Falls in the 1940s and 1950s. Hundreds of families were eventually forced to abandon their homes due to dioxin contamination of the land and water.

Confronted with government regulation, the industries that produced these chemicals fought back using lobbyists and political action committees. Their collective position was that the cost of environmental protection cannot be borne by chemical companies without making production uneconomical. With less money left for investment in research and development, there would be less innovation. Society will suffer. What manufacturers really wanted was to keep the economic costs of environmental damage and cleanup off their balance sheets and on the backs of taxpayers.

When the industry lobby's messages were played back to the public, though, what we heard was a slogan: "The solution to pollution is dilution." No need to spend money cleaning up the effluents from manufacturing processes and burdening manufacturers with cleanup costs. Mixing enough air and water with pollutants reduces toxicity enough to make them nontoxic. But this policy did not take into account that many pollutants are extremely toxic and tend to concentrate in the food chain. As the economy grew, the sheer quantity of pollutants quickly overwhelmed the environment; there simply isn't enough air and water to dilute the volume of pollutants produced to make all of it nontoxic. Worse, allowing corporations to externalize the social costs of pollution made their businesses appear more profitable than they actually were when all the costs are taken into account, leading to, in effect, a taxpayer-sponsored boom in certain manufacturing businesses that were otherwise uneconomical.

Today, no one believes that dilution is a practical approach by government regulators to protect the environment and the public from the chemical pollutants. Yet that principle was the essence of the government's regulation of financial innovations produced by the lending industry during more than two decades of the growth of the FIRE Economy. The by-product of lending is credit risk: financial innovations such as collateralized debt obligations—the equivalent of financial dioxin.

These products were supposed to spread credit default risk far and wide, diluting the toxic quality of the risk that lenders were taking on. As trillions of dollars worth of credit securities were created and sold to back mortgage, credit card, and other debt, credit risk toxins poured into the global financial system like dioxins into Love Canal forty years ago.

In early 2006, I wrote "Credit Risk Pollution," an article warning readers of an impending credit-risk Love Canal and of the need for financial rescue funds to clean up the financial markets after decades of credit risk pollution, equivalent to the superfund created in the United States to clean up the environmental mess made by decades of industrial pollution. Right on schedule, in the first quarter of 2007, the crisis in the global credit system occurred in the market for securitized mortgage debt. Soon it was discovered that credit risk pollution had poisoned the entire global credit system. Credit markets seized up. Banks went under. Governments poured money into the banks to try to get the credit markets working again. The United States created no fewer than six funds to clean up toxic debts by taking them off the balance sheets of financial institutions. The Troubled Asset Relief Fund (TARP) is perhaps the most well known.

All of this was as expected, except the global taxpayer-financed superfund for cleanup that I had called for never developed. Instead, each country affected has attempted to bail out lending institutions on a national basis, with the result that the only bonds that the markets trusted were government bonds and the highest-rated corporate debt. As a result, the global economy crashed even harder and faster than during the collapse of the credit bubble in the 1930s.

Why did regulators allow this situation to develop? For reasons that were very similar to those that created the industrial pollution crisis decades earlier, namely, the capture of regulatory processes by the very industries that were being regulated.

CAPTURE: THE SYSTEMIC CORRUPTION OF OUR INSTITUTIONS AND GOVERNMENT

To influence regulatory decisions, companies in an industry form trade associations to focus enormous sums on lobbyists and attorneys, in the hopes of reducing the impact of regulations by watering them down, by reducing the regulator's ability to enforce regulations, or, in the best case scenario, by abolishing regulations entirely.

Economists have a term to describe the dysfunctional relationship that can develop between an industry and the institutions that are supposed to be regulating them in the public interest: regulatory capture. But as the FIRE Economy evolved, not only were regulators influenced by the industries they were supposed to be watching, conflicts of interest between many groups that traditionally provide checks and balances broke down. This resulted in a convergence of interests across a broad range of institutions to the benefit of the FIRE industries at the expense of the general public and the productive economy. Professional economists working for Wall Street firms, central banks, financial institutions, commercial banks, and in academia adopted theories, such as that trade deficits don't matter, which over time became the new orthodoxy. Theory developed into a belief system that distinguished insiders from outsiders; the former got the jobs and speaking engagements, the latter were largely shut out.

In the end, the entire U.S. government became beholden to FIRE Economy interests, with respect to policy as well as intellectually. It didn't matter what party a politician belonged to: The entire economy had become systemically corrupt through the influence of special interest groups over public policy.

THE FALLACY MACHINE

How did everyone get it so wrong? How did the FIRE Economy develop right under our noses? How did Americans, traditionally thrifty and debt averse, fall into the debt trap?

The primary product of the FIRE Economy is debt, and debt is sold like any other product—with appeals to our emotions. Since the advertising industry began to follow the advice of advertising and public relations genius Edward Louis Bernays in the 1950s, physical products have been marketed to the public with increasing sophistication. Advertisers appeal to our emotions, not our rational selves. Cars are not sold on features and benefits, by amount of horsepower or seating capacity. They are sold by appealing to more essential desires—for power, prestige, and dominance—and only secondarily for safety and reliability.

A compelling example of the combined impact of emotion-based advertising and regulatory capture is the tobacco industry. Not that long ago cigarette smoking symbolized adulthood, independence, and sophistication, and few people considered smoking particularly dangerous.

The dangers of smoking were known for a hundred years before the U.S. Surgeon General's warning about the dangers of smoking appeared on packs of cigarettes. For decades, Big Tobacco conducted a highly effective campaign to prevent U.S. government health organizations from reporting independent medical findings, or from acting on them. Tobacco companies advertised in medical journals. Most movie stars smoked—the ultimate product placement. Not until reports of literally thousands of deaths and class-actions lawsuits did Big Tobacco's influence over government regulators decline. Today smoking is not only known to be unhealthy, but in our now more health-conscious society, smoking has become socially unacceptable, the habit of self-destructive addicts.

As Elizabeth Warren, Harvard Law professor, leading expert on consumer debt, and chair of the congressional oversight panel created to oversee the U.S. bank bailout, explained to me in an interview, "No credit card company ever ran an ad on television claiming, 'We sell the best debt.' Instead they show images of people enjoying what they purchased with credit cards—vacations or gifts—then they show a picture of a credit card. You know, for the best things in life, there's debt. They show a mother buying an expensive child seat for her car using her credit card. The message is that if you do not buy the child seat you are not a good mother, and as the audience can't afford to buy them with cash, the credit card company is selling the ability for a woman to be a good mother by using the credit card to buy the product. The ultimate message is that good parents take on debt."

Of course, this is backward, a fallacy. Good parents do not take on debts that they cannot repay. To do so is irresponsible. The FIRE Economy establishment was expert at selling fallacies that encouraged U.S. households and consumers to buy the product—debt—in quantities that posed a danger to the health of their household balance sheets, much as Big Tobacco sold the public on the benefits, and downplayed the risks, of smoking decades before.

How did these fallacies become embedded in the American psyche as deeply held beliefs? The fallacy machine has five parts: a germ of truth, an emotional hook, advertising with high production values, recommendations by "experts" in positions of authority, and repetition. In our chapter on beliefs we look into the workings of the fallacy machine in detail.

EIGHT FALLACIES OF THE FIRE ECONOMY

The FIRE Economy was built on a foundation of eight politically convenient economic fallacies.

1. A house is an investment.
2. Asset price inflation is saving.
3. Credit card and mortgage debt is safe.
4. The United States can grow its way out of debt.
5. Markets are efficient.
6. Chaos is freedom.
7. Financial success is luck.
8. Transparency is honesty.

1. A house is an investment.

Prior to the 1980s, it had always been well understood that the land is the investment, not the structures sitting on that land. Historically, a building had been a way of earning income from land in the form of rents; the other primary form of income from land was farming. A building was an expense, a depreciating asset requiring constant spending on maintenance to maintain its value. Only if a landlord could charge rent in excess of mortgage, maintenance, and taxes could a building make money.

Professor Robert Shiller, in the second edition of his book *Irratio-*

nal Exuberance, demonstrated that housing prices in the United States increased for the hundred years since 1900 only at the rate of inflation, with the exception of the post–World War I period, when pent-up demand resulted in an infrequent national increase in home prices. The only other instance of a period when housing prices outstripped income growth nationally was during the 2002 to 2006 housing bubble. Two years later I wrote a *Harper's* article in which I forecast a $10 trillion loss in home price inflation created by the housing bubble as prices reverted to the mean. The real estate Web site Zillow.com reported on December 15, 2008, that U.S. homes lost $2 trillion in value in the first three quarters of 2008. Total declines since the top of the market in 2006 are estimated at $3 trillion. By my estimates, the total value of U.S. residential real estate has a further $7 trillion to go over the next few years. When the process is over, homeowners will be severely disabused of the fallacy that a home is an investment.

2. Asset price inflation is saving.

During periods of asset price inflation in real estate and stocks—financed by credit expansion—households stop saving in the traditional sense of putting cash in a savings account and allow the asset price inflation to "do the saving for them." In the case of Japan, the asset price inflation period lasted from 1975, when the household savings rate peaked, until 1990, when the bubble broke. In 1990, the household savings rate increased for two years as consumers repaid old debt more quickly than they took on new debt, but has since resumed its decline.

Note that the Fed and Bank of Japan statisticians count repayment of debt as "saving." However, that saving does not go back into the economy. In 1991, the savings rate continued to decline even as households paid down debt. Households paid down debt but were unable to build up cash. In the case of the United States, the asset price inflation period began in 1980 with the birth of the FIRE Economy and ended in 2006 with the crash of the housing bubble. Savings rates in the United

States declined over the same period. My forecast is that, as in the case of Japan, household savings rates in the United States will continue to decline during the transitional economy. While Americans are coming to terms in 2009 with the fact that what they considered their "savings," based on stock and housing price inflation, have been wiped out by the housing and stock market crashes, they will find saving exceedingly difficult due to rising unemployment and falling incomes. Commentators who forecast that the increase in the savings rate at the end of 2008 presaged a long-term increase in household savings were mistaken. By 2010 it will reverse trend and resume the long decline interrupted by the recession.

3. Credit card and mortgage debt is safe.

American culture has been debt averse since the nation's founding. America, more than any other country, has stood for personal liberty, and escape from debt peonage was one of the motives for millions of immigrants to leave their home countries to come to the United States—to own their own property and be free of debt. Yet millions of Americans came to accept debt peonage over the past thirty years, during the rise of the FIRE Economy; they bought depreciating assets such as autos and appliances on credit although, in an earlier era, cash from savings was considered the only financially sound way to buy these items. Americans' attitudes toward debt not only became relaxed but turned upside down. A house, never considered an investment before the 1980s, developed into a mythic source of wealth, even though prices, as Professor Shiller demonstrated, did not rise faster than the rate of inflation—until the FIRE Economy era, that is. The magic of home price appreciation during the FIRE Economy era was accomplished via asset price inflation, which in turn was accomplished with low interest rates—which were thanks to foreign lending, and the foreign purchases of mortgage securities that backed those loans, and to subsidies from the government-backed mortgage companies Fannie Mae and Freddie Mac.

In 2009 Americans began what will be a decade-long readjustment to the old virtues of avoiding debt. Bankruptcy rates among formerly well-off American families are rising, and an entire generation will grow up under the hardships that excessive indebtedness causes, and will learn to be a debt-averse generation not unlike the one that the Great Depression spawned.

4. The United States can grow its way out of debt.

Warnings about government debt are as old as the debt itself, but what is often missed is the danger of the combination of high levels of domestic debt—that is, debt the United States owes to itself—and foreign debt—debt that the United States owes to other countries. The dangers of persistent government debt were well understood by our nation's founders. When Thomas Jefferson wrote in a July 12, 1816, letter to Samuel Kercheval, "We must not let our rulers load us with perpetual debt," he only echoed the counsel of rulers over the centuries. Roman, statesman, philosopher, political theorist, and lawyer Marcus Tullius Cicero warned in 55 BC, "The national budget must be balanced. The public debt must be reduced; the arrogance of the authorities must be moderated and controlled. Payments to foreign governments must be reduced, if the nation doesn't want to go bankrupt. People must again learn to work, instead of living on public assistance." Historians mark the beginning of the end of many great nations with the assumption of foreign and domestic debt that proved beyond the government's capacity to repay. In *The Republic* Greek philosopher Plato makes the case for a historical pattern of society devolving from democracy to anarchy to dictatorship to oligarchy with high levels of debt as the leading edge of the process. The debt-financed FIRE Economy is a modern infection by an ancient disease.

First the trouble comes in the form of perverse incentives. Why work hard to develop differentiated value as a country to earn export income when you can borrow other nations' savings to finance consumption and pay for government spending?

Next comes the worry of foreign creditors, concerned that they will find themselves second in line for repayment if the borrowing country starts to run into trouble paying all of its creditors.

Finally comes the day of reckoning, when the borrower cannot pay its debts and finance the operations of its government. A self-reinforcing debt deflation sets in. Foreign creditors, worried that they will not be repaid, force repayment, which creates the very crisis they are hoping to avoid by creating illiquidity in the market for the borrower's bonds. The bond market crashes, interest rates spike, and the economy of the debtor experiences a crisis that is referred to as a "sudden stop"—when output collapses.

To avoid this outcome the United States must both freeze debt growth and maintain its ability to service its existing debt. This will be very difficult to accomplish when debt levels of households remain high from the FIRE Economy era.

Vice president Dick Cheney famously told former treasury secretary Paul H. O'Neill that "deficits don't matter." In the coming years the United States will belatedly rediscover the old truth that fiscal deficits do matter, as the revenues needed to pay back the debt remain below the level needed to roll over the existing debt, never mind finance new debt needed to pay for spending programs to stimulate the economy, as the Japanese learned was necessary in the decade that followed the collapse of their stock market and real estate bubbles from 1990 to 1993.

5. Markets are efficient.

FIRE Economy economic orthodoxy claimed that markets are all knowing and that asset prices reflect knowable pricing information. The mantra of buy and hold, delivered with the consistency of religious belief, is this: You cannot time the markets. The buy-and-hold investor will see the best investment performance. Conveniently, this meant stockholders wouldn't sell regardless of performance. Believing this fallacy cost U.S. households $11 trillion in net worth, over $100,000 for the average American household. Thanks to poor net worth distribution in the United States, about 80 percent of those losses were concentrated in the top 10 percent of net worth groups, so that the lower 90 percent only experienced the loss as a brief decline in luxury goods purchases.

6. Chaos is freedom.

Lightly regulated markets operate more efficiently than heavily controlled markets. That portion of FIRE Economy free-market ideology is supported by history, but as with many valid principles, FIRE Economy ideology took the principle to the absurd. Regulatory institutions designed to promote the orderly function of markets were overrun by people and ideas that rolled the clock back to the 1920s' laissez-faire market era, before the lessons of the Great Depression were learned.

Government plays a critical role in markets. A market is like a highway of money. Consider your morning commute on a highway without lanes, speed limits or police enforcing them, repairs to potholes or the taxes to pay for them, or restrictions that keep trucks from overloading and spilling rocks or steel bars onto the road ahead of you. You can find such conditions in many third world countries, where the institutions that set and enforce the rules of the road are weak. When accidents inevitably occur there, emergency teams come to the rescue of the most prominent and wealthy commuters, leaving everyone else to fend for themselves.

That anyone might choose to intentionally turn a safe and well-regulated highway system into the dilapidated third world version might strike you as absurd, but that is precisely what FIRE Economy economic ideology argued was needed by U.S. financial markets.

Just as a highway free of lanes and speed limits and police is not truly free, our debt markets, for example, have become dominated by the will of the largest and fastest drivers, pushing as hard and as fast as they can in competition with each other, weaving in and out among the rest of us as we poke along with our mundane consumer and business borrowing needs, and as they use rarefied securitized debt instruments to fund uneconomical leveraged buyouts and mortgage loans, inevitably leading to the kind of massive slow-motion pileup that started in early 2007. By 2009, consumers and businesses were left trying to squeeze by in the credit market breakdown lane while passing the wreckage created by the crash of the securitized debt market.

7. Financial success is luck.

The FIRE Economy produced a lottery culture dominated by the belief that getting rich and "making it" are for the lucky and well connected, and that the way to get rich is through various forms of gambling, from trading stocks to buying and flipping houses to playing blackjack at a casino. Chance and relationships with insiders determine success. The lottery culture grew because the value of persistence, diligence, honesty, and competence—the virtues of a productive economy— faded in the face of the enormous winnings that financial players were able to reap. Why grind out a living delivering products and services? Go where the real money is: finance. In the 1980s the states jumped on the fantasy bandwagon, with lotteries, as well.

8. Transparency is honesty.

Enron practiced "transparency" to the letter, but not its spirit. Transparency is an embroidered version of the more simple term "reporting." Enron produced mountains of financial documents but the documents contained lies. The company did not fail because of shortage of reporting but because of a lack of honesty, of truthful reporting. The same is true of the ratings agencies when they issued their assessment of the risks of securities that backed subprime mortgages. The bond ratings purport to provide transparency by revealing the risks of loss to the bond buyer. In practice the ratings agencies delivered good ratings on bad assets in return for fees paid by the bond issuers themselves.

Transparency is easy to create and enforce by regulators setting reporting rules for institutions. The Securities and Exchange Commission, for example, imposes a complex set of rules on public companies so that investors have the vital information they need to assess a company's prospects. Honesty has proven more difficult to enforce. Even when financial fraud is proven, convictions are rare. Clearly, transparency is not the problem. Lack of motivation to be honest is the problem.

THE RUINS OF THE FIRE ECONOMY

At the end of the run-up to the near collapse of the world economy in 2008, what did the legacy of the FIRE economy leave us?

- unprecedented distortions in wealth, income, and debt distribution, leading to political divides between rich and poor, creditors and debtors, older and younger generations, and different races that will widen dangerously during the Great Recession, thwarting needed cooperation;
- high levels of domestic private debt, leading to onerous claims on the future cash flow of households and businesses;
- high levels of domestic public debt, which the debtor class owes to the creditor class, potentially creating deep internal political rifts between, for example, home owners and bankers;
- foreign public debt that leads to politically unserviceable claims on U.S. economic surplus and assets and potential loss of sovereignty over currency and interest rates;
- state and local government debt, which leads to bond defaults and municipal bankruptcies;
- state and local budgets inflated by high property tax revenues when home prices were inflated, leading to drastic reductions in services and government employment as property prices collapse and property tax revenues implode;
- depleted savings, which means households quickly deplete what little savings they have if one or both earners become unemployed

or underemployed, increasing the burden on government in the form of extended unemployment benefits;

- the crowding out of productive industries by FIRE Economy industries, resulting in crippled productive capacity (less than 50 percent of GDP), diminished export capacity (less than 20 percent of GDP), financialized productive industries (e.g., GM as a bank that makes cars), and a legacy of high medical, tuition, and insurance costs;

- an overvalued dollar, resulting in a third world–level transportation, energy, and communications infrastructure, foreign energy dependency, high energy intensity (too many BTUs—British thermal units—required to produce a dollar of GDP growth), and a threat of a sudden disruptive devaluation.

LONG-TERM OUTCOMES

After economists became aware in the 1990s of the credit bubble that had been developing in the FIRE Economy since the early 1980s, three distinct credit-bubble-collapse outcome camps formed: believers that the United States will experience either deflation, stagflation, or hyperinflation.

Deflationists believed that the coming credit bubble collapse was destined to turn into a deflation spiral, as the credit bubble did in the 1930s, with asset, goods, and wage prices all falling, leading to a "liquidity trap" and a self-reinforcing cycle of a collapse in the money supply, credit, and demand. They believed that the Fed's effort to reinflate the economy via expansion of credit and the money supply, and deficit spending, was doomed to failure. The heart of their argument was that the Fed cannot substitute enough government money and credit fast enough to compensate for the loss of private market money and credit as the credit bubble and economy collapse, and that the Fed lacks the mandate to support asset prices, such as by buying assets directly.

My position was that the liquidity trap and deflation spiral outcome was not possible, because central banks today have the option of printing unlimited amounts of money by the simple expedient of double-entry bookkeeping. Without the constraint of the gold standard that hampered money supply growth in countries such as the United States that stayed on it during the early years of the Great Depression, the balance sheets of central banks can be expanded virtually infinitely to compensate for losses in the private credit and money markets.

And so it was in 2008 and 2009. If a liquidity trap and deflation spiral was going to occur after the credit-bubble crash, early 2009 was the moment. That outcome was avoided by unprecedented action by central banks, including the purchase of distressed assets under an alphabet soup of programs, such as the TARP.

The early months of 2009 disproved the deflation theory. Going forward, two theories remain active, of those who expect hyperinflation and those who foresee stagflation.

Hyperinflationists believe that central bank and government actions to reinflate the money supply and support the economy with deficit spending, while successful at ending the immediate crisis that followed the collapse of the credit bubble, will eventually succeed in destroying the world's confidence in the currencies of those nations that pursued these policies. As the recession drags on, nominal tax revenues will decline, governments will become less creditworthy, economic output will stagnate or fall, and government will lose the ability to fund "sticky" budget liabilities. These include expenditures that cannot be cut for security or legal reasons, such as military expenditure during times of war and legal obligations, like government pensions.

Although the federal government can print money and finance expenditures with tax collections or by selling more government debt to domestic or foreign creditors, most states can neither print money nor run deficits and so must balance their budgets, and will do so by laying off government workers and raising taxes, actions that reduce rather than increase economic activity and output, at least in the short run, potentially creating a downward spiral if businesses are not able to grow to create new jobs. In this scenario, the federal government eventually has to print money without an offset of new federal government debt in order to pay expenses that it cannot cover with taxes or fresh borrowing.

Slowly—at least at first—the purchasing power of tax revenue will fall, so that even more money has to be printed simply to pay the bills. Interest rates rise as bondholders demand compensation for the loss in purchasing power. The economy slows even more, and with it tax collections. A classic hyperinflation cycle sets in, with the prices of goods and wages skyrocketing. Imports stagnate, and domestic consumers can no longer afford to buy them with their demolished currency. The inflation cycle only ends when the government raises interest rates far above the inflation rate and pegs the currency to an external anchor, such as another, more stable nation's currency, or land or gold.

In 1999 I developed what I call the "ka-poom theory" to model a U.S. version of the hyperinflation scenario. Most hyperinflation theorists foresee a doomsday when the United States' foreign lenders suddenly begin to sell their U.S. Treasury bond holdings. But if they do that, the dollar will weaken on global currency markets as dollars are exchanged for domestic creditors' currencies. The weaker dollar deflates the foreign debt; that is, the United States is allowed to repay it with cheaper dollars. At the same time, U.S. exporters get a competitive trade advantage over many of the very same creditors. The more the dollar deflates, the more the debt deflates, the cheaper U.S. exports become, the better the United States is able to compete with its trade partners that finance U.S. trade deficits.

If U.S. foreign creditors sell U.S. bonds because they are worried about a U.S. debt and dollar crisis, they will cause the very crisis that they fear. Smaller economies, such as those of Argentina or Iceland, that are at the periphery of the global trade system have indeed experienced this type of crisis, a kind of "run on the bank" that occurs as foreign lenders try to beat each other for the exits before their holdings in the country lose all value. As a group they cause the crash they are trying to escape. But the United States is not Argentina or Iceland.

The United States is the world's largest economy. What do U.S. lenders do instead? They buy even more U.S. debt to prevent a run on the bank cycle from setting in. The virtuous cycle of foreign borrowing and domestic consumption continues, at least as long as U.S. trade partners can maintain it. But what happens if a political or economic accident occurs and lenders to the United States cannot keep the system going?

Ka-poom theory envisions a U.S. sudden-stop disaster scenario. If a crisis occurs that suddenly and unexpectedly prevents China, Japan, and all other U.S. lenders collectively from meeting U.S. borrowing needs, the dollar will fall, U.S. interest rates and inflation will shoot up, and economic output will collapse. It is important to understand that in the U.S. case, such a crisis is a political and not a market event, resulting from a political repudiation of the United States and the U.S.-centric monetary and trade regime.

I see this scenario as highly unlikely but not impossible for the United States. The probability is high enough to warrant an investment in gold and the government bonds of net energy exporting countries to hedge the risk of a sudden dollar crisis. These belong in the portfolio in any case because of the implications of peak cheap oil because they serve a dual role of hedging the unlikely dollar hyperinflation scenario and the inevitable consequences of persistently high and rising oil prices over the coming decades. A more likely event than a sudden stop for the United States is a more gradual process in which the United States loses its central role in the world economy, and as a result its monopoly on the issuance of the world's reserve currency and its ability to borrow entirely in dollars. Americans in the United States will experience the process as a gradual and continuous decline in living standards as the dollar weakens, energy import prices rise, and high energy costs work their way into the prices of intermediate and finished goods. At the same time, unemployment will remain relatively high, so wages will not rise as quickly as goods prices in the economy. In fact, if you are living in the United States and paying attention, you have already experienced this dynamic for over two years.

This leads us to the stagflation theory—and the one I subscribe to as the most likely scenario for the United States, although a sudden stop remains a possibility worth hedging, however remote.

Stagflationists predict a middle road. They assume no operational or policy limitation to the Fed's and Treasury's abilities to expand the money supply, to substitute government credit for private credit as private debts are moved to the public account via asset purchases and so-called job creation programs. But they foresee, as the consequence of these policies, a weakening dollar and a stagnating economy, as government borrowing crowds out private borrowing, the private sector shrinks relative to the public sector, and government debt accumulates. The net result will be persistently high unemployment, flat or falling wages, and rising commodity and energy prices. This is the camp I have been in since 1998, when I founded iTulip.com to warn about the long-term consequences of allowing bubbles to develop. It will be the inexorable outcome of public and private overindebtedness that is the legacy of the FIRE Economy combined with the global dynamics of peak cheap oil.

The underlying post–credit bubble macroeconomic challenge is excessive debt—private and public, foreign and domestic—left over from the credit-dependent FIRE Economy. The U.S. economy has to get rid of a large portion of the remaining debt so that it can move forward again. But the phrase "get rid of the debt," as simple as it sounds, is the most politically charged of the new century, because to write off a debt means to not repay a creditor's loan, to take a loss on the asset on the other side of the ledger. To write off our foreign debt, for example, is to ask the Chinese, Japanese, Saudis, and Russians, and other creditors to take a loss on loans to the United States that were purchased with the savings of the respective nations' people. Asking them, in essence, to bail us out by eating our mistakes. Within these countries such a decision may become politically unacceptable, especially if economies weaken again in a fresh crisis, as I expect will happen at some point during the next peak cheap oil cycle. When another oil price spike sets off another global recession; no politician can accept a write-off of the people's hard-

THE POSTCATASTROPHE ECONOMY

earned savings at a time when savings are dear. In this scenario, the United States can't pay, and the creditors can't forgive.

That's where we stand. Over the past thirty years we have built up an economy on debt, an inflated currency, and oil. In chapter 2, we'll turn to the worldwide ramifications of the U.S. FIRE Economy and its fall: the transitional economy that we're living through right now.

CHAPTER 2

—

THE TRANSITIONAL ECONOMY AND FEEDBACK LOOPS

It is my guiding confession that I believe the greatest error in economics is in seeing the economy as a stable, immutable structure.

—JOHN KENNETH GALBRAITH,
   A JOURNEY THROUGH ECONOMIC TIME (1994)

The collapse of the FIRE Economy leaves the United States and the world facing dire economic challenges. At the time of this writing the recession that began in the fourth quarter of 2007 in the United States has mutated into a recession that came to be known as the Great Recession, as economies around the world reel from the combination of a crash in U.S. consumption and a decline in global credit. As most of Asia recovers, Europe and the United States fail to convalesce.

The choppy transition between FIRE and TECI is marked by economic contraction, punctuated by occasional periods of growth that is driven by fiscal stimulus spending. The National Bureau of Economic Research, a private, nonpartisan group based in Cambridge, Massachusetts, sets generally accepted start and end dates for recessions and expansions. On December 1, 2008, the bureau announced that the

United States economy had entered a recession on December 1, 2007. The bureau describes a recession as follows:

> a significant decline in economic activity spread across the economy, lasting more than a few months, normally visible in real GDP, real income, employment, industrial production, and wholesale-retail sales. A recession begins just after the economy reaches a peak of activity and ends as the economy reaches its trough. Between trough and peak, the economy is in an expansion. Expansion is the normal state of the economy; most recessions are brief and they have been rare in recent decades. The postwar average [length], excluding the 2001 recession, is eleven months.

An economic slowdown can occur for many reasons without developing into a recession. For example, after the attacks on the United States on September 11, 2001, economic activity slowed in the United States for a brief period, as consumers held up purchases, but it recovered within a few months. Economic activity in New York City, however, continued to suffer for over a year, in a regional recession. Regional recessions are common and are usually related to industry-specific events, such as the crash of the technology bubble in the early 2000s. Unemployment spiked in areas where technology companies accounted for a significant portion of employment, as companies closed and laid off workers. The San Francisco metropolitan area, for example, experienced a peak of 25 percent unemployment in 2003.

Similarly, Houston's unemployment rates rocketed during the Texas oil bust in the early 1980s that followed the inflation-induced oil boom of the late 1970s, as oil-related businesses went under. A regional Houston housing boom came to an abrupt end; housing prices plunged and home foreclosures reached historic levels, much as is happening in many regions of the United States today. In fact, the Houston boom and bust was prelude to the kind of employment and housing crisis we are now seeing in many states across the United States, such as Florida, California, and Nevada; those states experienced the highest rates of home price appreciation during the 2002 to 2006 housing bubble and also lack diversified economies that would redeploy the unemployed in new industries locally.

While it follows many of the same patterns as those that came before it, the Great Recession caused by the collapse of the FIRE Economy is unusual in both its national character and its global nature. During every other recession since the Great Depression, when one industry, like technology or energy, or an area of the country—Texas, say, or Florida—experiences economic decline, workers flee. They flee to new local industries or to areas of the country where another industry is growing. While the exodus from the region will tend to accelerate the downturn in the region experiencing the outmigration, this mobility provides a critical safety valve for the U.S. economy as a whole. The multiregional character of the U.S. economy is one of its unique strengths. Even if one region is doing poorly, another is usually growing, helping to pull the nation out of recession. The fifty states act as hikers roped together. When one or several slip and fall, the others pull to keep the whole chain of hikers moving forward.

But what if nearly every industry is contracting and laying off workers in every state? Then the entire country gets into economic trouble and the United States experiences a nationwide recession. Even so, a nation can still grow its way out of trouble. In the early 1990s, for instance, Japan took steps to cope with the recession that gripped the entire country in the wake of a collapsed bubble economy, using a combination of fiscal stimuli and policies that boosted exports to the rest of the world, and especially to the United States. (While this worked in the short term, it set the country up for serious trouble later.) In our case, the United States has counted on foreign borrowing to get the nation out of a national economic rut. Unfortunately, that era has come to a close. The United States faces an unprecedented challenge: It cannot borrow its way out of trouble as it has in the past, nor can it quickly export its way to prosperity, not during the period of the transitional economy, when the world economy is barely growing.

In addition to the extraordinary national U.S. downturn, major portions of the world economy are in crisis. Such a deep and widespread global economic downturn has not occurred since the end of World War II—and hasn't happened since the Great Depression, the last time so many countries experienced national recessions at the same time. Here are a few statistics from major economies around the world:

- According to the Japanese Ministry of Economy, Trade and Industry, industrial production fell 9.1 percent in January 2009, after falling 9.6 percent in December 2008, and it is estimated to have declined another 4.7 percent in February 2009. Japan's 34 percent decline in the five months starting in October 2008 exceeded the total decline in production during the entire three-year period of economic contraction that presaged the Great Depression.
- According to the National Bureau of Statistics of China (NBS), exports fell 17.5 percent in January 2009 from a year earlier. Imports plummeted 43 percent, as Chinese factories bought less foreign raw materials and consumer demand weakened.
- The European Union's statistical agency, Eurostat, reported that GDP contracted by 2 percent in Germany during the fourth quarter and by at least 1.2 percent for the sixteen-nation euro zone, an estimated annualized decline of about 5.2 percent in 2009.
- The U.S. economy shrank at an annual rate of 3.8 percent during the fourth quarter of 2008.
- The Bank of England reported that British GDP shrank by 1.5 percent in the fourth quarter of 2008 after a contraction of 0.6 percent in the third, and it forecast a "deep recession" in 2009, expecting it to shrink by 4 percent to 6 percent in the middle of 2009 from its level twelve months earlier.

Subsequently, the only major economy that reported significant GDP growth in 2009—in response to more than $2.2 trillion in global stimulus spending during the end of 2008 and early 2009—was China, and many observers were skeptical. Selected items from China's NBS Output and Growth Rate of Major Industrial Products report for November 2008 raises questions:

- carrier communication equipment: off 61.1 percent
- internal combustion engines: off 45.5 percent
- small tractors: off 41.2 percent
- fax machines: off 29.7 percent
- freezers: off 25.5 percent
- electricity: off 9.1 percent

The line item economic data is inconsistent with the official government reports of robust economic growth. Further contributing to the confusion, China does not account for GDP the way that most other countries do. Due to lack of consistency and transparency of economic data collection and reporting by China's economic statisticians, no one really knows how well China's economy is performing overall.

It's clear that when the U.S. FIRE Economy collapsed starting in 2007, it brought the world economy down with it. That was not how it was supposed to go.

Only six months before the economic catastrophe became obvious, toward the end of 2007, most economists believed that the world had "decoupled" from the U.S. economy. At a party put on by a hedge fund in the middle of 2007, a number of hedge fund managers lectured me about the poor prospects for the United States compared to Brazil, Russia, India, and China—the so-called BRIC nations—that were supposedly immune to any potential economic downturn in the United States. My own idea, which I presented as the keynote speaker at the Hard Assets Investment Conference in Las Vegas in August 2007 (but first proposed in 2005 in an internal presentation created for the venture capital firm Trident Capital), was that the collapse of the U.S. finance-based economy was likely to produce a U.S.-centric crisis that would quickly spread to U.S. trade partners. They are likely to recover first, however. In other words, decoupling of other countries from the U.S. economy has not happened yet—but will occur in the future as a consequence of the crisis.

When a global credit bubble collapses, a global debt deflation follows. Asset prices fall and the credit markets freeze up, as collateral values fall in price against existing debts, reducing creditors' ability to extend new loans. Credit contraction in the FIRE Economy then spills over into the productive economy, as occurred in the United States in the 1930s and Japan starting in the 1990s. When that happens on a global basis, there is a sudden withdrawal of credit-based purchasing power from businesses and households, and subsequently a global recession.

Suffice it to say, not only was the world not decoupled from the United States before the collapse of the FIRE Economy, it was as dependent as ever on the United States for demand. When the portion of demand supplied by credit came to a halt in 2008, so did U.S. demand; export-based economies from China to Dubai went into a tailspin.

NO PLACE TO HIDE

The international quality of the aftermath of the Great Recession presents unique challenges for any nation that are at least as serious as the period of contraction itself. In 1933, the U.S. economy stopped its severe contraction that started in 1930, yet no one claims that the Great Depression ended in 1933. Most historians believe that depression did not end until the early years of World War II when the per capita real income finally recovered to pre-depression levels. Similarly, the economic contraction phase of the Great Recession that began in the third quarter of 2007 ended two years later in the third quarter of 2009. While the contraction phase of the Great Recession ended in 2009, per capita income remains well below prerecession levels, particularly for the households in the lower 80 percent income group.

Under the structure of the global economy that developed during the period of globalization, countries cannot rely on each other as before. The United States cannot borrow from trade partners that are not receiving orders for goods from the United States. The United States acted as a primary source of demand for Japanese exports, for example, in the nearly two decades since the collapse of the Japanese bubble economy in 1990. How will Japan recover from the U.S. contraction? Who can Japan export to if not the United States? The answer is China. But if China becomes Japan's primary export partner, why should the Japanese continue to lend money to the United States? The answer is that Japan won't.

Within the United States, the transitional economy struggles with several interacting feedback loops kicked off by the collapse of the FIRE Economy. The first started with falling consumer demand for goods and services, which led to declining sales, which led to layoffs, which led to falling incomes, feeding back once more into falling consumer demand. But given the prolonged nature of our current crisis, this is only the beginning.

ECONOMIC FEEDBACK LOOPS

An economic depression can be thought of as a set of feedback loops that under normal circumstances do not develop to the stage where they become self-reinforcing. In every recession since the end of World War II, Keynesian government interventions in the form of interest rate cuts, tax cuts, and changes in lending policies have restarted the credit cycle to stop the process of debt deflation from feeding into an economic depression. In an economic depression, the government intervention in the credit cycle fails, and two major economic feedback loops develop.

Consumer-Employment Loop

1. falling consumer demand
2. falling business revenues and profits

3. layoffs

4. declining consumer purchasing power from income

5. go back to number 1

Financial Crisis/Consumer and Business Credit Loop

1. financial crisis

2. credit crunch

3. falling consumer and business access to credit

4. declining consumer and business purchasing power from credit

5. go back to number 1

In the case of the collapse of the FIRE Economy due to overall over-indebtedness of households and businesses, the consumer-employment and financial crisis/consumer and business credit loops feed into each other, creating a self-reinforcing megaloop that only ends when the source is eliminated—the overhang of debt.

U.S. FEEDBACK LOOPS

First, let's be clear: The transitional economy is an economic depression. Unlike a recession, which responds to monetary stimuli by a central bank, the process of an economic depression is prolonged, as debt is deflated either by a decrease in the monetary unit of debt—the currency—which happened from 1975 to 1980, during a relatively minor episode in the United States, or by default and deflation—the Great Depression of the 1930s. A depression is a prolonged affair that produces far more unemployment than a recession, and not only more unemployed workers but workers who remain unemployed for many years, years during which elections take place. Unlike a recession, which only produces a feedback loop of falling demand—as households reduce spending, businesses lay people off, unemployment increases, and demand falls further—a depression produces another feedback loop, between the electoral and economic processes.

Large numbers of unemployed vote for politicians who promise jobs, extended unemployment insurance, tax cuts, and other forms of relief. In the United States, this translates into political demands to grow an already huge public debt, while economic growth runs in reverse and tax revenues fall. The public sector begins to crowd out the private sector, as industries that employ large numbers of citizens, such as the automobile industry, receive support. The entire economy then becomes restructured around public spending. The result can be an economy like the United States at the end of the 1930s and Japan's today, one dependent on a ongoing series of fiscal stimuli measures, in perpetuity, to maintain economic growth. Voters demand that the government "create jobs" even though the government can only move jobs from the future to the present. Only the private sector can create jobs.

Alternatively—and this is our opportunity—the inevitable political impulse for the government to create jobs can be diverted to making investments in human capital and physical infrastructure long neglected and crowded out during the FIRE Economy era; government spending during the period of the transitional economy can lay the foundation for a self-sustaining TECI Economy.

INTERNATIONAL FEEDBACK LOOPS: THE GLOBAL CIRCULAR FIRING SQUAD

At the start of 2009, the global economic picture was dire, with many goods-exporting countries experiencing major declines in output and GDP and levels of unemployment not seen for generations. After the extraordinary stimuli that were applied in 2008 and 2009, the world economy stabilized, although the engine of growth in previous recessions, the U.S. economy, showed only tepid and tentative signs of recovery.

As of 2010, China stood out as a beacon of hope for global economic growth after the crisis. China, the world's third-largest economy, reported 8.3 percent growth during 2009 and predicted growth in excess of 10 percent in 2010. But two factors warrant caution for any-one who is pinning global recovery on China's continued blistering pace of expansion.

The first problem with the China growth story is that its official economic data are questionable, and much of the reported economic growth may not be real. Critics of U.S. Bureau of Labor Statistics data collection and reporting can safely accept U.S. economic performance data as positively pristine compared to China's National Bureau of Statistics.

For example, when the central government transfers money to a local municipality as part of its economic stimulus, the money that sits in an account of that municipality is counted toward GDP even if it is not spent and is not financing economic activity. Another example is the difference between the way that retail sales is measured in China compared to the United States and most other countries. In the United States, retail sales is a measure of money spent by consumers on products made by producers and sold through retail stores. China, in contrast, reports sales of goods sold by producers to wholesalers and other intermediaries as retail sales. The goods may sit in a warehouse but still be counted as a measure of consumer demand for goods made by producers.

Attempts to compare NBS line items from one period to another will frustrate the effort of anyone trying to get a handle on their economy. For example, automobile production was not a category in the February 2009 report of December 2008 industrial production data. This measure appeared in the March 2009 report and showed a 22 percent year over year increase. Yet in the same report, production of internal combustion engines, presumably a critical component of autos, was off more than 50 percent year over year in the February 2009 report of the December 2008 data, but that line item disappeared in the March 2009 report. Instead, a more general category of "engines" is listed, and it is off a more modest 7.8 percent. Unless Chinese automakers have been able to sell a large number of domestically produced autos without engines in them, the data simply make no sense.

Skepticism about the true nature of China's stunning economic performance following the global economic crisis and the government's response to it will cloud the global recovery picture in 2010, and adventuresome fund managers may bet against China by shorting its equity markets.

The second issue with relying on China to lead global economic growth for the foreseeable future is that the economy's performance, even if it is half as good as reported, is not sustainable. I refer to China's miraculous growth between 2007 and the end of 2009 as a "Greenspan credit bubble with Chinese characteristics." An accounting of bank credit and the money supply explain much of the so-called miracle.

The size of the stimulus that the Chinese government unleashed on its economy was greater than any other nation's after the crisis, nearly 7 percent of GDP versus 5.5 percent for the United States. Not surprisingly, this unusually large injection of government money into the economy had a large impact on the money supply and property prices a year later. A narrow measure of the money supply, called M1, made up of cash and checking accounts, increased a stunning 32 percent in the year that followed the stimulus, compared to 6 percent in the United States. Home prices increased in 70 percent of China's cities, even as home prices fell 12 percent across the United States, more than in any other year since the Great Depression.

The U.S. effort to reinflate the economy in 2009 paled beside the Chinese government's programs to stimulate consumer demand. The Cash for Clunkers program boosted U.S. car sales for two months, from a level so low that, on a unit sales basis, fewer cars were sold in the United States in 2009 than were sold in the worst period of the 1980s recessions, when the economy was one-third the size. Not in China. There auto imports grew at double-digit rates while they plunged nearly 50 percent in the United States.

In early 2010, talk of property and other asset bubbles in China prompted the government to do as the United States did in 1999 and 2000, and in Japan ten years before in 1989. By mid-2010 China's government will attempt to begin the process of gingerly withdrawing credit and money to try to cool the economy and create a soft landing. The lesson learned is that bubbles don't have soft landings, no matter how long the government drags out the process or how many warnings it issues. China's economy is due to pop, just like any other, once the government takes the punch bowl away. When it does, investors with money in China will try to get it back out again. But China does not buy into the notion of free capital flows, and foreign investors will likely see their funds held in China until the crisis blows over. For that reason, the outcome will not be as disruptive to the financial system as the U.S. crisis, but it will leave the world without a single dominant source of demand. Instead, the drivers of global recovery will be spread among many so-called emerging economies.

Recovery will not immediately improve the unemployment picture in the United States, and the political-economic feedback loops will take on a life of their own, with consequences that are impossible to foretell.

Because the world economy is not decoupled from the U.S. economy, the collapse of the FIRE Economy is having unexpected worldwide implications in the developed and emerging-market economies. These old classifications of undeveloped, emerging, and developed will be replaced in the post–FIRE Economy and peak cheap oil era by a new way of measuring relative economic strength and potential: as net energy exporting creditor nations and net energy importing debtor nations. For the foreseeable future, the former will have the upper hand over the latter, but the transition will not be seamless.

Starting with the non-OECD nations, growth will be slow during the transitional economy because most of them are export-based, especially China, and the primary demand engine for the world, the United States, will not be fulfilling that function as it was before the crisis. Trade among Asian countries and between Asia and non-U.S. regions, such as Europe and Latin America, will grow even as trade with the United States stagnates.

The debt hangover of the FIRE Economy in the United States, combined with persistent high unemployment and declining income, as well as the negative wealth effects of declining stock and housing prices, will motivate households and businesses to save more and pay down debt. Governments will fight this tendency by attempting to stimulate households and businesses through purchases of debt securities that the private markets are avoiding and policies such as quantitative easing—also known as "printing money"—in order to prevent a 1930s-type general price deflation.

DEFLATION: MAKING SURE "IT" DOESN'T HAPPEN HERE

When he was a little-known economics professor at Princeton University, six years before the great crash of 2008 and four years before he was appointed head of the Federal Reserve, Ben Bernanke made what became a famous speech. Even though no one had asked aloud, he answered the question on the minds of all thoughtful policy makers who observed the explosion of public and private debt that followed the bailout of the U.S. economy after the collapse of the stock market bubble two years before. The speech was titled "Deflation: Making Sure 'It' Doesn't Happen Here."

In that speech, Bernanke assured his audience—mostly of individuals and representatives of institutions with a vested interest in the FIRE Economy—that the Fed stood ready to apply every tried and true monetary tool (and a dozen untested and experimental methods as well) to avoid a repeat of 1930s deflation. The speech presupposed the condition of overindebtedness that raised the specter of a 1930s-style economic crash, but Bernanke didn't discuss that. Bernanke is a scholar of the Great Depression era who wrote numerous papers on the subject since the early 1980s, but he never mentioned the shared antecedents of the two eras—overindebtedness and debt deflation—and the risks they posed. He believed from his reading of history that a self-reinforcing series of crises could follow from a liquidity trap, creating a cascade of falling asset and commodity prices and menacing the overindebted U.S. economy with a repeat of the 1930s Great Depression.

In his 2002 speech, Bernanke said, "I am confident that the Fed would take whatever means necessary to prevent significant deflation in the United States and, moreover, that the U.S. central bank, in cooperation with other parts of the government as needed, has sufficient policy instruments to ensure that any deflation that might occur would be both mild and brief."

Various traditional efforts by governments to stimulate debt-laden economies will result in brief periods of apparent recovery. This is what happened in the United States under New Deal programs from 1934 until a new depression hit in 1938, after fiscal stimuli were temporarily reduced as a result of political pressure to reduce deficits. A similar cycle of stop-and-go fiscal stimuli in Japan followed the collapse of Japan's asset-bubble economy in 1990. Each time the government tried to reduce government spending, the economy fell back into recession about a year later.

Stock markets will rally during the periods when fiscal stimuli and new credit and money creation appear to be working. After decades of struggling to recover from its twin stock and property bubbles, and from pursuing economic policies designed to avoid repudiation of private debt that grew during the credit-bubble era, Japan will exceed its government debt threshold and finally succumb to a long overdue debt crisis. In the end, the policy of moving private debts to public account, to deleverage the private sector using the public sector's credit, will prove a failure, this despite the immense creativity and hard work of the Japanese people. The U.S. experience from the 1930s is inconclusive, because World War II interrupted America's second depression. One post–credit bubble mistake is certain to happen again, just as the original sin of allowing a credit bubble was repeated: In the midterm election year of 2010 the fiscal deficits, upon which the U.S. economy has come to rely to prevent private sector debt deflation, will be a political football for the foreseeble future, just as it was in the United States in the 1930s until World War II and in Japan since 1996. The result of politically motivated cuts in government spending, or pressure for austerity measures from United States creditors will be a fall-back into recession in 2011. The stock market will see it coming by late 2010, and decline precipitously. Alternatively, if deficit spending continues, the economy may continue to muddle along into the 2012 U.S. presidential election. In that case, oil demand will expand to reach another production limit as we saw in 2005 that, together with a weakening dollar, led to the rapid oil price increase from 2006 to 2008. A similar rise will produce a second recession by 2013 if one is not induced sooner by spending cuts.

The global downturn that started in 2007 will continue as long as the source—that is, unpayable private and public sector debt—is not addressed constructively. Government economic policy makers will try desperately to engineer economic recovery with one fiscal stimulus package after another, and radical monetary policies in addition to 0 percent interest rates, including the printing of money without a balancing issuance of new debt, a practice called "quantitative easing." The United States will try nontraditional economic stimulus policies once the traditional monetary stimulus measures of lowering interest rates prove effective after short-term rates approach zero and there is nowhere for the Fed to go. Collectively these policies are referred to as Zero Interest Rate Policy or ZIRP. In early 2009, the central banks of the United States, the UK, Canada, and others began to experiment with so-called quantitative easing, as Japan did in the early 2000s, in an attempt to exit a liquidity trap that can occur in a 0 percent interest rate environment.

An economic downturn of an economy struggling with excessive debt is also referred to as a "balance sheet recession" because excessive debt on the balance sheets of households and businesses is consuming cash flows and thwarting recovery. In a 2008 presentation Japanese economist Richard Koo warned policy makers in the United States that monetary stimulus will not be effective to stop a balance sheet recession in the United States. The lesson of Japan is that such a recession only responds to fiscal stimulus because the money supply does not expand fast enough through private borrowing to increase the money supply when the balance sheets of households and businesses are already overburdened with debt. The economy becomes dependent on government spending to grow the money supply. He warned that a letup in spending will quickly translate into a money supply decline and a resumption of deflationary processes: insolvency, business failures, and rising unemployment.

In late 2008, a panic out of stocks, bonds, and other securities denominated in the currencies of the previously fast-growing economies of Russia, India, and others produced a rush for U.S. Treasury debt and dollars. But the desperate attempt by the Treasury and Federal Reserve to protect the financial and banking industry firms from losses— through programs that purchased securities outright or arranged for government guarantees of securities purchased by private parties— will erode confidence in the soundness of U.S. sovereign credit and of the U.S. dollar.

These monetary and fiscal stimulus policies worked in the past, during all previous global crises since the early 1980s, because each of those crises began at the periphery of the global economic system that revolved around the U.S. FIRE Economy. The U.S. FIRE Economy was the basis for the global financial system and for economic stability; when the U.S. recovered, all other affected countries soon followed. The difference with the current global crisis is crucial: This time it emanates from the United States and has thrown the rest of the world into disarray; they cannot rely on the U.S. economy to stimulate recovery. During the acute crisis phase of the collapse of global finance that the FIRE Economy spurred, the dollar gained strength, but each country, OECD and non-OECD alike, now faces its own unique economic and political drama.

Economic policy makers worldwide have no model for a global crisis centered in the United States. Solutions that worked well to address the economic crisis for one country at a time when other countries are still growing are counterproductive when all nations are facing economic decline in one form or another. Worst of all is the reflex to borrow the economy out of debt, following the doomed orthodoxy of modern central banking in periods of crisis.

Overindebted consumers cannot borrow their way out of debt; a major portion of the debt needs to be forgiven, especially mortgage debt. Instead, the U.S. policy makers will try to maintain the flow of debt payments to banks and financial institutions from households that lacked sufficient income to qualify for a mortgage during the housing bubble boom; during the economic bust that follows, those households are even less able to repay debt. In 2009, more than 60 percent of government-sponsored home mortgage refinancings failed for this reason.

The political motivations for these policies are clear. Politicians have to appeal to voters who will otherwise be foreclosed on by banks, and to their primary campaign contributors, who are captive to FIRE Economy interests. The tendency of politicians to try to bribe voters with jobs and extended unemployment insurance leads to all manner of dysfunctional decision making, such as efforts to prop up badly managed automobile companies such as General Motors at the expense of well-run ones such as Ford.

Since the crisis began in early 2007, the U.S. government has done everything it can to avoid taking the obvious steps needed to get the U.S. banking system working again. All it needs to do, as the Norwegian government did in the 1990s (and the U.S. government itself did during the savings-and-loan crisis of the late 1980s), is: create a Resolution Trust Corporation–type bank holding company, send a team of accountants in to determine the solvency of all banks that hold asset-backed mortgage securities and other unmarketable securities, put the insolvent banks into receivership, transfer their assets to the holding company, sell these assets to well-run solvent banks, and move on. The longer U.S. politicians protect campaign contributors from losses by using taxpayer money to provide capital to and purchase assets from companies that failed the test of the market, the longer insolvent banks will clog up the U.S. banking system, the longer the crisis will continue, and the more the collapse in private credit markets will prolong the subpar growth that characterizes the transitional economy. The longer bank executives who made mistakes are allowed to continue to run them, the longer the road to recovery of confidence in the U.S. banking system.

The FIRE Economy and the credit boom it created ended in the second quarter of 2007. The sheer scale of the debt created by that boom has made the debt deflation unmanageable by traditional methods of credit crisis management. In 2008, for the first time since the 1930s, the world economy faced the threat of global monetary deflation, with asset price deflation spilling over into the real economy and driving down commodity prices. Such a collapse in the prices of loan collateral worldwide, from commercial buildings to houses, reinforced the insolvency in the household, corporate, and financial sectors of major economies where property markets formerly boomed, such as the United States, the UK, Ireland, and Australia. At first monetary policy was employed to try to stop the process, but central banks quickly ran short-term interest rates down to 0 percent as asset prices kept falling.

Governments spent trillions to support the mortgage market to reinflate housing first and commercial real estate prices later. Normally, asset prices would be allowed to decline, which would attract new buyers; attempts by governments to stop the decline only prolong the pain, as similar policies have in Japan since the 1990s.

Starting in the final quarter of 2008, national governments worldwide attempted to blunt the impact of the recession on employment and production through fiscal stimulus programs meant to spark recovery. In addition to large scale experiments with radical monetary policies, such as quantitative easing, many governments abandoned their past fear of developing outsized structural budget deficits as they increased public spending outlays, even as tax revenues collapsed along with GDP declines. Ireland, the United States, and the UK flirted with fiscal deficits that in boom times were considered third world levels, in excess of 10 percent of GDP in 2009 and 2010. In early 2010 the congressional budget office projected a budget deficit of more than 10 percent in 2011. Given its past forecasting track record, that estimate is likely to be low. In early 2008 the CBO forecast a budget deficit of around 4 percent for 2009; in reality it turned out to be 13.2 percent.

The urgency for economic policy makers to appear activist in 2009 was compounded by the timing of the recession. Hastily forged fiscal packages were pushed through the legislative process with little discussion. Legislators hope for "multiplier effects" of fiscal spending, but multiplier effects only result when a dollar spent now by the government to create jobs will allow workers to pay more than one dollar of tax revenue from income. Unfortunately, the spending was so rushed and haphazard, and so driven by pork-barrel politics, that a dollar of spending is producing a dollar of new public sector debt but a negligible increase in output and jobs. For the most part, governments may have done better to throw the money out of helicopters as Fed chair Ben Bernanke once suggested in a speech in 2002 on approaches to preventing a second Great Depression, clearly a worry even then.

Many countries nationalized major parts of their financial systems. In March 2009, ex–Fed chairman Paul Volcker said, "We're in a government-dependent financial system; I never thought I would live to see the day. . . . We've got to fight to get away from that." The net result of taking on so much debt while increasing outlays is a global explosion in fiscal deficits. The relative fiscal debt positions of various countries will play out as an important factor in determining currency values when peak cheap oil, covered in chapter 5, exerts the next wave of recessionary forces on global economies.

Countries like the United States that depend on continuous inflows of foreign capital to finance both fiscal and trade deficits run into serious trouble when trade partners, such as China and Japan, can no longer lend as much as before because output and exports are falling. In February 2009, for example, Japan's exports fell 49 percent year over year. With the domestic economy imploding, where will Japan get the money to buy U.S. Treasury and other debt? The United States will have to print money and buy its own debt, and in March 2009 the Federal Reserve started to do just that. By the end of 2009, only China was left standing as a buyer of U.S. debt. Without tax revenues and foreign borrowing, the United States faces a cash-flow crisis that may result in a sudden stop: a sudden reversal of capital flows as foreign private holders of U.S. financial assets sell them to move money out of the country, resulting in rising interest rates and inflation, further slowing the economy.

DEGLOBALIZATION

The domestic political challenges created by high unemployment and energy prices will tend to sideline joint interests among trade partners. The result is a kind of national political narcissism, a plain response to economic crisis at home that puts abstract international principles behind immediate national economic needs. High-minded ideals of eradicating poverty and improving the environment well tend to give way to more mundane domestic priorities, such as feeding the poor, who will be hurt the most by expensive oil and will increase in numbers rapidly as oil becomes more scarce. The phrase commonly used in this phase of the transitional economy is "economic nationalism," and it refers to the short-term policy decisions that politicians make to try to protect their constituencies, especially from the effects of high unemployment. These policies may take the form of protectionism, that is, laws that protect workers from foreign competition.

If the United States does not reform its financial markets and economy, in the coming years a popular election platform in many countries will be the promise of trade and other policies that distance them from the United States. This is the political expression of the process of deglobalization that will result if the United States remains on its current course. The United States will become economically isolated and global capital inflows that have financed job growth for decades will diminish as a percentage of global GDP.

Early in the global economic crisis that started with the collapse of the U.S. FIRE Economy in 2007, the leadership of several small European governments was replaced by voters due directly or indirectly to global economic stresses. The government of Iceland was an early casualty, followed by the governments of Latvia and the Czech Republic. Similar overthrows of incumbents will occur wherever unemployment remains high. Greece and Spain are high on the list of countries that are likely to experience political instability, followed by Japan.

Parts of Eastern Europe developed a particularly unstable FIRE Economy of their own between 2001 and 2007, borrowing $1.7 trillion abroad, much in short-term debt. In 2009 the region needed to repay 23 percent of that total, or $400 billion, nearly a third of the region's GDP. Even under the best of circumstances, refinancing such a quantity of private debt is difficult; with the global credit markets shut down, the task is virtually impossible.

Russia is stuck with $500 billion in private debts from loans used to finance its oil industry during the oil boom that developed while the dollar depreciated 40 percent between 2002 and 2008; oil prices rocketed to $147 a barrel in 2008. With oil trading at $50 a barrel less than a year later—half the price assumed in its national budget—the debts cannot be repaid. Fearing a repeat of the Russian bond crisis that occurred in 1998, investors sold ruble-denominated debt. Russia bled 36 percent of its foreign currency reserves in a few months, after the crisis hit in September 2008, in its attempts to defend the ruble. The ruble later stabilized, but only because oil prices rebounded sharply from March 2009 panic lows.

In Poland, 60 percent of mortgages are borrowed from Swiss banks and denominated in Swiss francs. When its currency, the zloty, declined by 50 percent against the franc in the winter of 2008, adjustable-rate mortgages didn't merely rise a few percentage points as they did in the United States; they doubled, and housing prices collapsed. All across Eastern Europe, from Latvia to Hungary, from the Balkans to the Baltic and Ukraine, the story of property bubbles repeats. While the United States was busy developing the subprime debacle, Eastern Europe created its own property bubble and mortgage lending crisis.

Unlike the U.S. banks, which borrow from other countries in dollars, the European banks left themselves liable to additional lending risks that go along with lending to another country that has to maintain sufficient currency reserves to repay foreign debts. Eastern European debts are owed to Western Europe—to Italian, Swedish, Austrian, Belgian, and Greek banks—in euros by countries outside the euro zone such as Latvia, which has to convert debt payment from its local currency, the Latvian lat, into euros. When these smaller debtor countries were hit by the global recession, exports and currency reserves dwindled at the same time the housing market, where the loans were concentrated, turned down and the loans soured. Europe's sovereign credit risk is not confined to risky loans to Eastern Europe. While U.S. investors bet heavily on emerging markets during the boom, European investors account for 75 percent of the $5 trillion portfolio of loans made to emerging markets since 2000. Spain invested heavily in Latin America. Britain and Switzerland invested in Iceland and Asia.

As bad as the U.S. financial system appears to be, Europe's is in some ways even worse off. The euro zone suffers from a structural flaw that the United States does not have. There is no central treasury authority for the European Union as there is in the United States, no "euro treasury department" that, together with the central bank, can act as a lender of last resort to flood the markets with liquidity; the EU is deflation prone because it cannot inflate debt as broadly and as rapidly as the United States can. This fact tends to make the euro stronger during the transitional economy period.

In 2010, the year after many Eastern European economies rolled over, currencies sank and interest rates soared, sovereign credit risks within the euro zone itself appeared. Greece was the first to default on foreign debt. The response of the euro zone was reminiscent of the early days of the subprime mortgage crisis in the United States in 2007, with half-baked measures to end the crisis and assertions that the risks are "contained." As of this writing, street rioting has erupted over austerity measures taken by the Greek government as demanded by creditors such as Germany who have reluctantly responded to the crisis with emergency loans. A second weakness in the euro zone structure was revealed by this event. The constituent nation states of the euro zone can accumulate external debts in a way that U.S. states cannot. The states of California and Illinois are experiencing budgetary crises as tax revenues dried up during the recession and remain below the level needed to finance liabilities, but to the extent that these liabilities are debts the risk is limited to municipal and other debt internal to the state. There is no risk of credit contagion among U.S. states. In the euro zone there is both contagion risk and lack of a central authority to respond to a credit crisis experienced by one or more constituent nation states.

The deflationary bias on the euro created by the lack of a central treasury and euro bond market pushes the euro up while the threat of a generalized euro debt crisis will tend to cause a flight to other currencies and push the euro down. How these two opposing forces will balance out is difficult to predict. An optimist will expect the euro leadership to work through the tactical problem of shoring up Greece and Spain before the crisis spreads. That leaves the deflationary force of a structural weakness in the architecture of the euro zone that prevents rapid euro debt expansion. The euro strengthens against the dollar in this scenario.

A pessimist will foresee European countries reverting to old nationalistic habits. Evidence of this appeared in Germany in March 2010 when Josef Schlarmann, a member of Angela Merkel's Christian Democrat party, suggested that Greece sell Greek islands to raise money to repay its debts. This did not go over well with the Greeks, who responded by invoking the Nazi occupation of the country during World War II. A serious diplomatic incident was only narrowly avoided. This revealed the bottom line difference between the euro and the dollar: the dollar is glued together by the federation of states, that in other countries might be called provinces, while the euro is held together by a collection of regulations and directives—treaties, laws, and court judgments—that define the euro zone. Each country has its own culture, history, and language. In good times when the global economy is expanding, such as from the inception of the euro in 1999 until the global crisis in 2007, the arrangement worked well. As the economic crisis that started in the United States in 2007 goes through stages of evolution, the durability of the euro zone will no doubt be put to further tests.

In Asia, Japan faced the worst crisis in its history when the economic crisis that started as a housing bubble collapse in the United States reached Japan in 2008. After nearly twenty years of postbubble economic stimuli, Japan's gross public debt approaches 200 percent of GDP, less than Zimbabwe but more than Jamaica. With a chronic domestic demand deficit due to having the oldest population of any country on earth—the middle-aged and elders consume little—and immigration policies that discourage young foreign workers from entering the country, dependent on exports for income, as exports crashed more rapidly than during the Great Depression, Japan appeared to be at the end of the road. The government undertook yet more stimuli so that the OECD projects will push Japan's deficit to 200 percent of GDP in 2010. Dylan Grice, a strategist at Société Générale, calculates that $2.4 trillion of government bonds, equal to 45 percent of the country's GDP, will mature and need to be refinanced in 2010. As weak as the euro and dollar appear to be, the Japanese yen may at some time in the next few years produce the largest currency dislocation since the Soros's fund sold short more than $10 billion worth of pounds sterling in 1992, forcing an official devaluation.

In China, government efforts to cover up the extent of its economic distress ran into trouble when reports of mass layoffs leaked out through unofficial channels. An unelected government gains legitimacy by providing for the economic needs of its people. If it cannot do that, it faces social and political turmoil. As more than 50 percent of China's toy and consumer electronics factories shut down, tens of millions of migrant Chinese factory workers returned to the countryside. Much like the hundreds of thousands of illegal immigrants who entered the United States through its southern border to build U.S. homes during the housing bubble between 2002 and 2008, and who returned home in 2009 after the jobs dried up, Chinese emigrants from the countryside returned home from the cities that previously had offered seemingly limitless opportunities. China, long relying on capital controls, export duties, and other measures to maintain neo-mercantilist policies to accumulate wealth, doubled down with export subsidies and the largest fiscal stimulus programs of any country on Earth in order to keep the economy growing and to maintain the flow of exports to the Americas and Europe.

In one important respect, China's unelected government is looking out for its people far more effectively than elected U.S. officials have. Chinese officials see peak cheap oil coming, and have for over ten years sought out relationships with natural resource– and energy-exporting countries around the world, from Africa to Latin America. Much as the United States used to do in the 1950s and 1960s, China invests in local infrastructure, builds schools and roads, and buys resource rights. For several years China has been stockpiling oil and other resources aggressively, as the reality of global resource constraints has been rapidly approaching. China is investing heavily in nuclear power, with plans to build more than thirty reactors over the next ten years. The global race for energy efficiency and reduced dependence on fossil fuels is on, but with only limited plans to expand nuclear energy, America isn't even in the game.

While political leaders preach free trade and globalization in word, they practice economic nationalism in action. America's hastily put together $790 billion fiscal stimulus plan included "Buy America" provisions, potentially in violation of the letter and certainly in violation of the spirit of World Trade Organization (WTO) rules.

Russia raised import restrictions on automobiles and farm machinery, Argentina imposed restrictive licensing requirements, Indonesia restricted the entry of competing firms, China imposed tighter quality standards and export restrictions, and India raised tariffs on imported steel, as did the European Union and Brazil.

Worldwide, automobile manufacturers represent a major source of employment; no government can sit by and allow the plight of thousands of voters to go unheeded. Governments in the United States, the UK, China, Brazil, and most of the euro zone countries provided financial assistance to struggling car companies. The Hungarian government provided subsidies to first-time car buyers.

As governments broke the bank to finance bailouts at home and to support domestic credit markets through purchases of debt securities, nations like the United States that rely on capital inflows to finance current account and fiscal deficits are forced to finance the shortfall. The United States became a net creditor for the first time in decades in the fourth quarter of 2008, not because it lent more but because foreign lending to the United States plummeted; the Federal Reserve made up the difference, buying the Treasury and agency debt itself. The hope is that net foreign investment will pick up again, as it has as part of every other recovery since the birth of the FIRE Economy in the early 1980s.

The economic nationalism practiced by countries coping with short-term crises may reinforce the devastating short-term effects of the transitional economy on trade and capital flows if the trend continues. Yet the trade, investment, financial markets, and supply chain interdependence of the world economy is well understood by governments. A repeat of the mistakes of the 1930s era is unlikely. But then regulatory and trade organizations are always fighting the last war.

Marginal protectionist measures that nations around the globe took during the early stages of the transitional economy conjure a modern-day re-creation of Smoot-Hawley, the 1930 protectionist bill credited with turning the 1930s panic into the Great Depression. But the protectionism of the future will not be an overt re-creation of the past. Rather it will manifest itself in a contest among nations to depreciate currencies to fight debt deflation and boost exports, with the most indebted—the United States—leading the pack because it needs a weaker dollar both to generate price inflation signals in the economy to counter the deflationary force of persistent unemployment due to ongoing credit market weakness and to increase the export sector of the economy to create jobs. Unlike in 1933 when the United States called in gold and repriced it by nearly 70 percent, effectively devaluing the dollar against gold by as much and producing a 40 percent surge in inflation over six months as import prices soared, this time the antideflation, export boosting policy was executed early and in a more gradual and covert manner. The dollar was allowed to depreciate due to large-scale Treasury issuance, low short-term interest rates, quantitative easing, and gigantic fiscal deficits, any of which weigh on the exchange rate value of any currency but in combination were guaranteed to weaken the dollar against the currencies of U.S. trade partners that did not take these measures. In the short run, the losers in this strategy, especially Europe and China, will tolerate it as a necessary policy for the United States to pursue to get its economy moving again. But if the policy continues for more than a year, China and Europe will begin to put pressure on the United States to take measures to strengthen the dollar, such as raising interest rates.

UNEMPLOYMENT LOOP

In total, the U.S. economy lost seven million jobs by the end of 2009, as unemployment shot up more than 10 percent. The unusual characteristic of the transitional economy is long-term unemployment. Many of the ten million unemployed produced by the Great Recession will remain out of work longer than at any time since the Great Depression. As of early 2010, median duration of unemployment—the measure of the length of time that the average unemployed American remained out of work—continued to rise to more than twenty weeks. The highest previous recorded level was twelve weeks during the early 1980s recessions. Even steeper job losses in a second recession brought on by the next peak cheap oil cycle cannot be ruled out, especially if other feedback loops intensify. For example, rising unemployment will lead to a further 20 percent to 40 percent decline in real estate prices between 2010 and 2012 as incomes decline. A further tightening of credit as the pool of credit-worthy borrowers contracts means even deeper losses in the wholesale trade sector, leading to more unemployment, and so on.

The proximate cause of the recession was the sudden disappearance of the purchasing power that had been created by the credit expansion in the U.S. economy beginning around 1980. Between 1980 and 2007, the U.S. economy went from needing a dollar of new private and public sector borrowing to produce a dollar of GDP growth to dependence on more than five dollars of new debt to generate a dollar of GDP growth. This credit growth, which temporarily fueled employment, was accomplished by various unsustainable means, including foreign borrowing, financial engineering, and leverage.

In 2008, after net capital inflows had slowed to a stop in 2007, launching a financial crisis and causing sudden stop economic effects, first the United States' and then international credit markets seized up. The U.S. government, through the Federal Reserve and Treasury Department, attempted to restart the flow of private credit in the United States—but with only limited success. The inexorable logic of American politics dictates that the next phase of economic remediation is direct substitution of government credit for private credit by lending directly to private firms, such as the loans to U.S. automobile makers. This lending will be broadly expanded throughout the economy during the transitional economy as the depression continues, with certain industries and sectors tending to benefit more than others and other unintended consequences drastically changing the structure of the U.S. economy.

The structure of proposed loans to U.S. auto manufacturers is the litmus test for government support of U.S. industries in the transitional economy. The crisis in the U.S. auto industry is the tip of the iceberg. Many other goods-producing and service industries will follow.

The backbone of the U.S. economy is not its large manufacturers but its many thousands of small goods and services businesses, the heart of the business innovation that drives the American economy. While politicians and pundits debate the bailouts of large financial and manufacturing companies, no one is speaking for the small businesses that not only maintain America's competitiveness but have traditionally pulled the U.S. economy out of recession in the past. Where is their bailout? The unintended consequence of dealing with insolvent employers on a first-come, first-served basis prioritized by size is that small innovative businesses will be less able to compete with large sclerotic corporations.

One thing leads to another. While future bailouts of private companies are likely to follow the pattern of the first, the U.S. taxpayer is not an infinite source of money. What set of principles should be used to prioritize and structure government assistance to private industry? What form should it take? The answer lies in the kind of economy we want after the economic crisis ends. Do we want an economy in five years dominated by a few large, internationally uncompetitive companies or a thriving ecosystem of small innovators that can improve American productivity, efficiency, and competitiveness?

The social consequences of the kind of mass unemployment that will occur during the transitional economy will, if not addressed by government stimuli, split the nation into competing interest groups by age, income group, and industry, groups that will fight for decades over a shrinking pie. The truly sad part is that the pie could be growing if all of these groups were working together to achieve a common goal: an efficient, competitive economy based on productivity, saving, and investment. Doing nothing is not an option. On the other hand, our course today, one of ad hoc bailouts going to the biggest, most vocal, and best politically connected, first in banking and then in the auto industry, will lead to an economy of big corporations and big government, and a decade or more of economic stagnation may follow.

A flawed economic stimulus policy from 2001 to 2003 produced the world's first fiscal stimulus program executed in reverse order— the housing bubble—with jobs first and government spending second. We don't need to pile another set of flawed government programs on to cope with the fallout from the last. America was built on innovation and trade. Bailouts of large companies need to be balanced with capital gains and income tax cuts that allow the dynamic sectors of the U.S. economy to continue to grow the economic pie for all.

Chapter 3 takes a closer look at the government's wrongheaded response, rising unemployment, and the role of inflation and explores whether a politics-free economics is possible.

CHAPTER 3

—

WRONGHEADED RESPONSE

Enormous dosages of monetary medicine continue to be administered and, before long, we will need to deal with their side effects. For now, most of those effects are invisible and could indeed remain latent for a long time. Still, their threat may be as ominous as that posed by the financial crisis itself.

—WARREN BUFFETT, AUGUST 2009

At the start of the debt collapse, the Federal Reserve and Treasury threw money in front of the avalanche in one desperate bid after another to hold back the cascading agglomeration of debt. The desperate effort to defeat the pitiless force of economic gravity failed by steps as the collapse gained speed. They redoubled the effort.

Interest rates were slashed from 5.25 percent in 2007 to 0.13 percent—effectively to 0 percent—in 2009, yet consumer and business borrowing continued to decline.

Trillions of dollars of central bank cash were injected into banks, yet the debt continued to deflate.

Currencies fluctuated, the dollar first rising savagely as investors fled emerging markets. Capital also fled the dollar to other safe havens,

—

such as hard assets, as governments used radical and unorthodox measures to battle price deflation with monetary measures designed to induce higher prices in the economy.

As the full mass of debt built up during the more than three decades of the FIRE Economy continued its relentless downward journey, governments launched ever more titanic fiscal stimulus programs in well-intentioned bids to restart stalled economies and reemploy millions of newly jobless, homeless, and hungry. Ad hoc and reflexive government responses continued, and one industry after another has lined up for emergency loans to stay afloat. The federal government tried to accommodate them to stem the surge of layoffs, but by the end of 2009 it finally confronted borrowing limits.

In 1990, at the start of its lost decade, before Japan doubled and redoubled its public debt, the world owed Japan hundreds of billions of dollars. But at the start of this crisis, when the United States embarked on a similar plan to combat its balance sheet recession by moving private debt to public account, the United States owed the world $13 trillion, an entire year's GDP. The United States had become like a spendthrift uncle who lived well by borrowing from his relatives during the boom. He's gambled it all away, and now he's back for more. But now some of his relatives have problems of their own.

In 2008, the United States had a gross external debt of 95 percent of GDP in 2008, the U.S. dollar traded near twenty-year lows, short-term interest rates hovered near 0 percent, and the economy is contracting (although it showed signs of life in the third quarter of 2009 in response to the extraordinary monetary and fiscal stimulus, which included multibillion-dollar programs directly subsidizing new car and first-time home purchases). The only tools left to get the U.S. economy growing again are the devaluation of the currency, to boost exports and deflate debt, and deficit spending. The former reduces the purchasing power of the return on the loans and the latter increases the risk of default.

The United States feels the full weight of outstanding foreign and domestic public and private debt. The Keynesian cure of deficit spending is the order of the day, with government creating demand to compensate for losses in the private sector. But how will new bonds be sold to raise the money needed to pay for these spending programs?

THE COMMON FATE OF DEBTORS

The FIRE Economy leaves the United States facing not one but three debt crises. First, after decades of buying homes and goods on credit, U.S. households have more debt than they can repay. Second, pension, Medicare, and Social Security liabilities are far in excess of income that the government can collect from taxes, borrowing, and interest without stifling the very economy that produces the money and credit for the government to collect on. Third, the debts of the federal government to the people and governments of other countries will prove painful to disengage from without subjecting the United States and its creditors to deep political and economic distress.

For the entirety of the FIRE Economy era, no U.S. president dared demand that its people and the government itself cut back on borrowing. Each crisis that resulted from a lack of cash flows from borrowing was met with a renewed wave of fresh borrowing from a new source, either a new foreign lender or a new market for debt within the United States itself. No leader urged "sacrifice today" to avert disaster tomorrow.

Any middle-class American couple with heavy debts that experiences job loss will tell you that there is no miracle cure for the condition of too much debt, limited savings, and not enough income. A nation can no more wish away debt than a husband and wife who borrowed $1 million to buy a home when times were good can wish away $10,000 monthly payments after one of them loses a job and their incomes together fall to less than the amount of the monthly mortgage alone—never mind food, tuition, or medical bills. After the couple burns through their savings, they have no choice but to try to renegotiate the debt with creditors, or default.

Private foreign holders of U.S. debt, made up of both Treasury bonds that finance the federal government and agency bonds that back home loans, became net sellers in 2003, selling more U.S. debt than they purchased. Drastic lowering of interest rates and the issuance of massive new debt, as well as the reinflation policies of the U.S. government in the years following the stock market crash of 2000, signaled to private markets the beginning of the end of the FIRE Economy. Private institutions and individuals en masse invested their money elsewhere, leaving the task of purchasing U.S. debt to maintain the foreign debt arm of the U.S. FIRE Economy to their government, referred to as "official" buyers in government reports.

The political policies of global central banks and the dollar cartel extended the old interdependence of the U.S. government and trade partners throughout the world, protecting the United States during the final years of the FIRE Economy. Today China is America's largest creditor, but China is only the most recent in a long string of codependents in dysfunctional arrangements with the debt-financed U.S. FIRE Economy and America's trade partners in Asia and the Middle East, who rely on foreign demand rather than their own internal consumer demand to fuel economic growth.

For the political leadership in Japan, Taiwan, and Saudi Arabia, for example, the quid pro quo of lending to the United States are variations on a theme: Lend to the United States and receive orders for exports of oil or consumer electronics from U.S. consumers as well as American military protection from enemies of the state. Your economy will grow, your people will prosper, and—most important—you will stay in power. But by the end of 2008, as the U.S. economy wallowed through its second year of contraction, U.S. consumers cut their purchases of foreign oil and goods. America was no longer keeping its side of the foreign lending bargain. The field of potential lenders to the United States diminished from dozens in the early 1980s to only one: China.

The principle of U.S. foreign borrowing was applied equally to democratically elected governments, like Japan's, and dictatorships in China and Saudi Arabia that see themselves as benevolent albeit unelected shepherds of their people. The human rights group Amnesty

International ranked these two regimes as the sixth and seventh most repressive on Earth in 2009, a political factor of creditor-debtor relations that will haunt America during the transitional economy.

The political benefits of lending to America during the FIRE Economy era will continue beyond the economic gains made during the transitional economy even though U.S. consumers will reduce their appetite for imports and the federal government will pursue policies to reduce American dependence on oil imports from its creditors. The geopolitical and military advantages of an alliance purchased by lending to the United States will remain, but the economic cost to America of upholding even that part of the bargain will shift in favor of less, not more, expenditure overseas to maintain its role as protector of geopolitical arrangements.

The virtuous cycle of borrowing and lending, spending and growth, that both reinforced America's power and its partnerships in Europe and across Asia will slow and may even reverse. America's ability to enforce terms of trade relations favorable to the West and a geopolitical order that favors the strong dollar and its corollary, cheap oil as priced in dollars, is giving way to the reality of America's dire fiscal crisis and the drawing down of the last of the world's good, inexpensively produced oil.

By the middle of 2009 even China's leadership began to get nervous. Upon his return from China, Richard Fisher, president of the Dallas Federal Reserve Bank, told the *Wall Street Journal* for a May 27, 2009, report: "Senior officials of the Chinese government grilled me about whether or not we are going to monetize the actions of our legislature. I must have been asked about that a hundred times in China. I was asked at every single meeting about our purchases of Treasuries. That seemed to be the principal preoccupation of those that were invested with their surpluses mostly in the United States."

In the years leading up to America's debt crisis, China busied itself spending its hoard of U.S. Treasury bonds to buy natural resources, such as iron ore, copper, and oil, for use as raw materials to build its burgeoning cities and towns. In the process, China shifted the risk of a U.S. debt restructuring or default onto the new countries holding U.S. debt—such as Africa and Latin America—usually as collateral against loans to China.

As the U.S. fiscal crisis continues, no one knows what the Chinese leadership will do, but even if they do no more than stop buying U.S. debt, interest rates in the United States will rise, some estimate by 1 percent or more per year. The U.S. FIRE Economy, like a shark that must swim to breathe, must continuously borrow from the pool of international savings in order to run its economy and government, and to maintain the value of its currency, the dollar. When it stops swimming, it starts to suffocate financially. A vicious cycle follows.

Between the challenge of maintaining demand for its currency and the impact of rising energy prices, deflation is the least of America's problems during the transitional economy. Instead, the result of overindebtedness and debt deflation may be a second period of inflation, similar in some ways to the inflationary period of the 1970s.

HOW CAN OVERINDEBTEDNESS AND DEBT DEFLATION LEAD TO INFLATION?

On the surface, the precrisis conditions of the United States in 1929 and 2006 appear similar. Deeply indebted households. Reliance on consumption for economic growth. Excessive risk taking in unregulated financial markets. A credit bubble. But there are two major differences. In 1929, the U.S. dollar was tied to gold, and the United States was a creditor, not a debtor, to foreign countries.

The primary cause of the extended deflationary spiral that afflicted the U.S. economy, and no other national economy in the 1930s, was strict adherence to the gold standard, which limited the ability of the central bank to expand the money supply.

Economists and economic historians, including Milton Friedman and Ben Bernanke, blamed the relatively poor performance of the United States during the Depression on the Hoover administration's fiscal and monetary conservatism in the early years of the crisis. The

Japanese monetary authorities and politicians were similarly criticized in the 1990s by economists such as Paul Krugman for making similar errors—for taking too long and doing too little to prevent a debt deflation from turning into a self-reinforcing deflation crisis.

Indeed, in the 1930s, nations that had just abandoned the gold standard, inflated the money supply, and executed aggressive government spending programs were struck less severely during the Depression. Unconstrained by a gold standard, the Bernanke Fed and the U.S. Congress applied what they believed were the lessons of the Great Depression in 2008 and 2009 and of Japan from the early 1990s. Economist Irving Fisher first described the debt-deflation in his 1934 paper "The Debt-Deflation Theory of Great Depressions" published in *Economietrica*, a now defunct economics journal.

> Each dollar of debt still unpaid becomes a bigger dollar, and if the overindebtedness with which we started was great enough, the liquidation of debts cannot keep up with the fall of prices which it causes. In that case, the liquidation defeats itself. While it diminishes the total number of dollars owed, it may not do so as fast as it increases the value of each dollar owed. Then, the very effort of individuals to lessen their burden of debts increases it, because of the mass effect of the stampede to liquidate in swelling each dollar owed. Then we have the great paradox which, I submit, is the chief secret of most, if not all, great depressions: The more the debtors pay, the more they owe. The more the economic boat tips, the more it tends to tip. It is not tending to right itself, but is capsizing.

An overindebted economy is like a poorly loaded ship with too much weight above the deck and not enough ballast. A financial crisis is a rogue wave that hits the ship from one side. The ship must be quickly righted before it tips to the point where it begins to capsize. The Fed must pump water into the hull to increase the ballast and at the same time counter the excess debt weight from above deck. It does this by making hundreds of billions of dollars in no-questions-asked loans to banks and by taking bad debts and unmarketable securities off the balance sheets of banks and onto its own. At the same time, aggressive government lending and spending programs grow the money supply before a self-reinforcing debt-deflation process—the capsizing of the economic ship—develops as a result of banks not lending and households not borrowing. As an indirect consequence of these policies, the dollar weakened relative to other currencies, providing an additional ship-righting force of cost-push inflation from energy import prices.

In the short run, these policies were successful. The United States experienced a brief two-month period of price deflation in early 2009, not forty continuous months as it did in the 1930s. By catching the debt-deflation process early and not allowing inflation to fall below zero for an extended period, the United States also escaped the stag-deflation that Japan has experienced since the early 1990s. Stag-deflation is the condition of a debt-laden economic ship that lists to one side for decades on end, drifting in and out of deflation and recession. Following the radical measures taken to right its economic ship, the United States will experience a completely different set of economic problems, neither listing nor capsizing. The net result of the policies was not only a redistribution of the debt, from private to public, from above to below deck, but an overall increase. The United States will ride low and slow in the water, barely able to move and vulnerable to being sunk outright.

The rescued United States economy is vulnerable to sinking because of the condition of foreign indebtedness that neither it nor Japan had before, during, or after earlier debt deflation episodes. Unlike the United States in the 1930s or Japan in the 1990s, before the financial crisis wave hit in 2007 the United States was not only not a creditor nation but a debtor. This is why policies designed to halt debt deflation directly through bank bailouts and fiscal stimulus also had the indirect effect of causing the dollar to weaken. This indirect benefit of U.S. foreign indebtedness, to allow trade partners to facilitate the depreciation of its currency, has built-in limitations. Fewer and fewer trade partners will be willing to play along. In the economic catastrophe that began in 2007, the United States was already down to a handful of reluctant major creditors from a wide field of eager lenders ten years before. By the end of 2009 it was down to three that made up more than 80 percent of net purchases of U.S. Treasury bonds: China, Japan, and the UK.

The United States is financially beholden to China, a country that the Pentagon considers America's number one military threat, to Japan, which recently elected a new government that ran on a platform of reforms designed to reduce Japan's economic and military dependence on the United States, and to the UK, which is in even worse economic trouble than the United States and which investor and currency speculator George Soros put on the top of the list of countries most likely to experience a debt and currency crisis in the near future. Yet foreign lending to the United States from these nations must continue if the FIRE Economy is to revive, even though America's damaged banking and financial systems, overindebted households, lack of productive capacity, and other legacies of the fall of the FIRE Economy remain.

Not likely.

THE SECOND GREAT INFLATION

The prices of commodities, goods, services, and wages fell drastically with the money supply throughout the U.S. economy from 1930 to 1933. When the administration of Franklin D. Roosevelt took over in 1933, its first move was to go off the gold standard and depreciate the dollar by nearly 70 percent against gold, then the primary international currency for trade, producing a surge of cost-push price inflation in the United States from rising import prices.

In 1933, Metro-Goldwyn-Mayer produced an educational film featuring Professor Gordon Watkins. The short, *Inflation Explained*, was played at movie theaters around the country that year. The movie made the case in ten minutes that inflation is good for business, the economy, and the country.

Fast-forward to 1979. The U.S. economy suffered the opposite monetary affliction, too much rather than too little inflation. The OPEC oil price shock and the profligate printing of money by the Nixon administration to pay for the Vietnam War and Lyndon Johnson's social programs generated an eight-year period of inflation that came to be known as the great inflation under the not-so-watchful or politically independent eye of Federal Reserve chairman Arthur Burns.

In the background, starting in the mid-1970s, future Fed chairman Paul Volcker engineered a new regime. Economist Milton Friedman played the role of academic economist front man by selling the idea that "inflation is always and everywhere a monetary phenomenon." Inflation arose from the government printing too much money. The solution: Shut down the government's printing press. Forty-five years after the FDR administration sold inflation to the public as the cure for a depression, the Reagan administration sold the public on deflation—and, as it turned out, two recessions—as a cure for inflation.

The Paul Volcker Fed raised interest rates to historically unprecedented levels, throwing the U.S. economy into a severe recession doubleheader. The objective of the plan was twofold: One, frighten investors out of non–interest bearing assets, such as land and commodities, and back into stocks and bonds sold by financial institutions. Two, break the wage-price inflation spiral that threatened by late 1979 to turn America's first great inflation into a hyperinflation.

A wage-price inflation spiral happens when wage rates feed back into goods and services prices. Wage earners demand, through political action—including through unions—wage increases indexed to inflation, increases in the minimum wage, and other policies that keep wages rising along with the prices of goods and services in the economy. A recession broke the wage-price spiral with double-digit unemployment. Without jobs, wage earners lost pricing power. The managements of companies in unionized industries threatened to go out of business if wage concessions were not made; many unions dissolved. The wage-price inflation feedback loop was broken, and inflation fell to low single digits, where it remained, at least officially, for the duration of the FIRE Economy.

A generation of economists came away from the experience of the early 1980s convinced of three points:

1. Without wage inflation, a wage-price spiral—and thus sustained inflation—cannot happen.
2. Management of wage inflation through monetary and government policy will prevent a recurrence of the late 1970s' style inflation spiral.
3. Inflation management could be done through an economic policy of wage price controls formed on the basis of outsourcing, liberal immigration laws, and an antilabor policy of a low minimum wage—all wrapped in a free-market ideology.

Inflation in the prices of financial assets, however, did not enter the FIRE Economy economist's policy field of vision. In fact, the Fed managed asset price inflation through an entirely different set of policies: They encouraged it by a combination of credit market deregulation, also wrapped in a free-market ideology, and neglect. The result was a series of asset bubbles starting with the leveraged buyout (LBO) bubble of the late 1980s, followed by the stock market bubble of the late 1990s, and ending with the housing bubble from 2002 to 2006.

Government will, through economists, sell the benefits of inflation or deflation, depending on circumstances and political expediency, but no one has to sell anyone on asset price inflation. Who can argue with rising home prices? The catastrophe happens on the down side of the bubble equation, but it's to no one's advantage to advertise that fact at the time.

Starting in 2006, collapsing bubbles led to asset price deflation. First housing prices fell, then securitized debt products crashed, then the stock market, then commercial real estate. The Fed got busy with the reinflation of asset prices through government lending programs, such as the Making Homes Affordable program designed to reduce home mortgage payments, and never before tried Fed programs to rescue banks, such as the TARP that resulted in the Fed adding more than $1 trillion in asset-backed securities and agency bonds onto its balance sheet. The Fed took ninety-five years to grow its liabilities from approximately $400 billion inflation-adjusted dollars at its founding in 1913 to $850 billion by 2008. With the addition of bad debts and unmarketable securities during the financial crisis that followed the collapse of the housing bubble, in less than one year the Fed's liabilities more than doubled to over $2.2 trillion. In late 2008 and early 2009 the Fed and Treasury lent trillions of dollars to banks, and trillions more were committed to government spending programs to get "the economy" going again—the FIRE Economy, that is. Authorities were not worried about inflation. The Bernanke Fed was busy making sure deflation didn't happen again.

Complacency about future inflation grew out of two fallacies: the legacy idea of the Volcker era that inflation cannot occur without wage inflation, and, should inflation arise as a result of the Fed's radical measures to stop it, the Fed can withdraw money by raising interest rates, quickly ending the inflation. Both assumptions will in the years to come be proven false.

Government money spent or lent to reinflate the FIRE Economy cannot be so quickly removed from the economy, because while the government can always rush liquidity—cash—into the economy after an asset bubble pops, it cannot control where all of the money goes. More important, inflation will serve politicians better than the alternative, just as it did in 1933. Lucky for them there are two inexorable sources of inflation that they can blame instead of themselves.

INFLATION WITHOUT WAGE INFLATION

Those who believe that recessions always put an end to inflation grew up in the era of Paul Volcker and Milton Friedman and the ingenious simplifications they formulated to sell a politically inconvenient but economically valid anti-inflation agenda, the mission accomplished by pushing short-term interest rates several points above the inflation rate: kill a wage-price inflation spiral by throwing the U.S. economy into recession, thereby raising unemployment and thus cutting wage earners' pricing power. Afterward, the FIRE Economy evolved as inflation and interest rates fell. Ever since then, throw a beer can out the window and chances are you will hit someone who believes three economic fallacies. One, when unemployment rises, inflation must fall. Two, monetary inflation acts on the prices of goods, services, commodities, and assets equally, and, conversely, if prices are rising, it is always due to the central bank issuing too much money—and to no other cause. Three, that the impact of inflation is always measurable by an increase in the general price level. We start by debunking this first misconception, that high unemployment necessarily leads to falling inflation.

Inflation is a purely monetary phenomenon—except when it's a currency value phenomenon. If the exchange rate value of a nation's currency is falling, that means that the prices of imports are rising. This fact is highly relevant for the United States and is about to become more so for two reasons. One, because the U.S. imports most of the oil it consumes, a falling dollar makes oil more expensive in the United States and in every country where oil is purchased in dollars, even if global demand is declining. The high cost of imported oil exerts a disproportionately large impact on the prices of competing goods. This is true of all imports. In fact, the prices of goods manufactured in the United States can be falling at the same time as imported goods prices are falling, provided the domestic goods do not compete with the imported goods. If they do, then the prices of those domestically made goods go up, too.

The idea that inflation is always and ever a monetary phenomenon also incorrectly assumes there is only one kind of money operating on all available goods, services, and assets in the economy. It is important to distinguish among different kinds of inflation and between goods and services prices versus asset prices. Different kinds of money, resulting from a range of kinds of borrowing, inflate the prices of goods and assets independently. A surplus in mortgage credit pushed up home prices but not commodity prices and wages for the simple reason that wages and commodities are not purchased with mortgage credit. In the future, expect to see asset prices continue to deflate while the prices of goods that are energy intensive to produce, such as food, rise. This will tend to squeeze U.S. households as incomes continue to stagnate. Only goods that rapidly increase in value due to technological innovation, such as consumer electronics, will tend to grow in both revenue and unit sales terms. Food sales will rise, as will gasoline sales, but mostly due to inflation, not because more units of gasoline and food are being sold. This combination of inflation in goods prices and deflation or stagnation in wages is commonly referred to as "stagflation," but it will not be like the stagflation of the 1970s, primarily because wage rates will not rise. It will be the United States version of the "stag deflation" that Japan has experienced since its credit bubble popped in the early 1990s, at least unless or until ka-poom happens, that is, a debt and currency crisis, or the politically inexpedient task of post–FIRE Economy debt restructuring begins. Americans will find that the impact of inflation is not always measurable as an increase in the general price level but can instead be exhibited by the subtle and less easily detected trend of declining product and service quality as the purchasing power of savings and incomes is gradually eroded by a persistently weak dollar. This is the long-term outcome of the Fed's successful effort to prevent debt deflation. The quality of many products, especially food, will diminish as cheaper inputs are substituted for more expensive ones. For example, rather than higher prices for restaurant meals, you can expect more a la carte items on the menus so that when you wind up with the same items on the plate that you had ten years ago total price will be considerably higher.

NO PLACE TO HIDE II: UNEMPLOYMENT BY STATE

In the spring of 2008, it looked like the boom might last forever—the boom created by a depreciating dollar, that is. Oil prices increased as the dollar weakened, and later in the cycle when hedge funds ran out of other assets to chase, they ran to commodities, especially oil, pushing the price to an incredible peak of $147. At the time, debate raged over whether oil price increases since 2004 were caused by dollar depreciation or increased demand from China, India, and other rapidly developing countries. By early 2009, it became apparent that $100 of the $147 oil price had been about 20 percent a factor of increased demand, 40 percent of dollar depreciation, and 40 percent speculation; by the end of February 2009, the price of oil was below $40.

Between mid-2006 and mid-2008, as the housing bubble took jobs away from the economies of states where housing prices had been inflated most, a weak dollar gave some of it back. States that are both housing bubble states and destinations for tourists, such as Florida, thrived on the tourist trade as Asians and Europeans came to spend their strong currencies at the U.S. fire sale. A euro goes a long way when it is trading $1.40 to $1.00. Even New York City was cheap to a tourist from Germany or France. With all of the foreign tourists, American cities, from Las Vegas to Los Angeles, became Towers of Babel.

States that produced oil and coal boomed like Houston in the 1970s, creating some unlikely state winners, such as South Dakota, if only briefly. Other states benefited indirectly, such as those that produced corn for ethanol, and agriculture generally boomed with commodities, as the weak dollar made U.S. exports cheap.

Alas, the weak dollar party came to a sudden end in the fall of 2008 as a spike in oil and commodity prices crashed credit markets already staggering from the collapse of the housing bubble. An intense few months of global deleveraging ensued. The hedge funds that had poured money into Russia, China, and other promising nations quickly sold assets denominated in rupees, rubles, pesos, and reals, and bought U.S. Treasury bonds denominated in dollars. The net result: a huge spike in the exchange rate value of the dollar and a collapse in commodity prices.

States that depended on a weak dollar to support energy and tourism industries were hit hard, and states that additionally enjoyed the housing boom experienced a double whammy.

Florida and Nevada are two economies that depended on the housing bubble, and then the weak dollar, for growth. After the housing bubble popped, these states' economies went into free fall.

- States that experienced the highest rates of home price appreciation during the bubble, including the housing bubble ground zero states of Florida and California, began to experience rapid economic contraction and unemployment growth in 2006 after a six- to twelve-month lag from the 2005 housing bubble peak.
- States with persistently high unemployment rates, over 7 percent, had not played in the housing bubble; therefore, the housing collapse nationally has had little direct impact on the local economies and unemployment in those states. However, the post–housing bubble recession is beginning to impact these states too, via reduced demand for output.
- States that are benefiting from high energy prices are seeing little impact from the collapse of the housing bubble because energy prices were low for years before, depressing economic activity in those states that in turn resulted in high unemployment rates, a showstopper for a statewide housing bubble.

SOLUTIONS TO THE UNEMPLOYMENT PROBLEM

The transitional economy began in earnest in October 2008. What could the government do to slow or stop the feedback loops that were reducing demand and creating unemployment in the U.S. economy? Was the loss of ten million jobs in the U.S. economy during the Great Recession inevitable?

The 2001 recession was shortened by the expedient of households borrowing against the inflating value of their homes, using cash-out refinancing of mortgage loans from 2002 to 2006. From the time that home prices started to fall in 2006, and credit began to tighten, no similar trick can be executed during the transitional economy to turn an illiquid asset like a house into cash. Rule changes to allow savers to tap their 401(k) and pension funds are in the works, but freeing up this relatively limited stock of illiquid savings cannot make much of a dent in the shortage of cash that is only just beginning to hit U.S. households. Half of U.S. households have no money in 401(k) or Keogh plans. The top 75 percent net worth group has only $15,000 in 401(k) funds. This is a paltry source of illiquid funds to make liquid compared to the $222,000 in home equity at the start of the 2001 recession that was available to tap via home equity loans. In 2010, home equity was declining due to falling home prices. Banks were cutting the availability of credit to a shrinking pool of credit-worthy borrowers. That left a relatively small reservoir of funds in retirement accounts that were devastated by a 20 percent decline in the stock market since 2007 as the primary source of savings for unemployed Americans to pay the bills. No wonder the government had to extend unemployment benefits three times in 2009 and 2010. There is no ready source of illiquid capital to convert to cash anywhere in sight. The long-term consequence of asset-inflation and indebtedness of households during the boom times of the FIRE Economy became the liability of taxpayers through unemployment insurance after the FIRE Economy went into crisis.

One of the extraordinary developments of the transitional economy will be an ongoing decline in consumer credit and lack of availability of loans to small businesses. The former will be reported incorrectly as a rising savings rate, as households repay debt more quickly than they take on new debt, but it will not represent an increase in liquid net worth that presages a rebound in consumer spending. Retail sales will appear to rise, but this will be due to inflation—retail sales data are not inflation-adjusted—as retailers who survived the downturn regain pricing power and charge more for food, gasoline, and other goods in industries that do not suffer from global overcapacity. Clothes, for example, will remain inexpensive for the foreseeable future but quality will suffer. Lack of access to credit by small businesses will prove to be the worst problem facing the nation, as small businesses are the usual source of new employment to allow the economy to expand and recover.

THE EXPORT SOLUTION

Since 2001, a weak dollar helped the United States grow export revenue by hundreds of billions of dollars per year from 2000 to 2008. With the dollar strengthening and global demand falling, that source of economic growth is no longer available during the transitional economy. U.S. policy makers may take measures to depreciate the dollar to increase inflation expectations, but the United States is out of monetary, currency, and credit tricks to play to halt the current recession to prevent it from turning into a depression. The only tools left are fiscal, and the sooner the United States deploys them, the better the chances that a depression can be avoided.

Professional economists did not forecast the financial crisis that began in 2007 that led to the collapse of the FIRE Economy. Their forecasts of the economy that has followed the crash have been far off as well. Why? Three reasons.

First, the FIRE Economy was finance-based. Few economists have a background in finance and do not understand the influence of it on the portion of the economy they know well, the one based on production and consumption. Economists, from the classicists, such as Adam Smith, David Ricardo, Thomas Malthus, and John Stuart Mill, to those of the Austrian School, such as Friedrich Hayek, to Keynesians, to monetarists such as Milton Friedman, all focused on the traditional matters of prices, output, income distribution, and money in markets and the forces of supply and demand. But the sum of all payments within the FIRE Economy—from the transactions of stocks, bonds, and other assets—is larger than all payments of wages, taxes, and invoices in the productive economy. If the FIRE Economy is by that measure larger than the productive economy, why aren't more economists trained to understand how it works, how they interact, and what it means to the future of America and the world? This is especially relevant since it has been crises in finance, that is, in the FIRE Economy, that have posed the greatest risk and created the largest economic crises of the past one hundred years. To the majority of economists, the FIRE Economy is not discussed, as if it did not exist. The one economist who has done the most rigorous and thorough research on the FIRE Economy, and can be said to have in fact identified FIRE Economy and coined the term, is Professor Michael Hudson, professor emeritus at the University of Missouri, St. Louis.

Second, the accepted economic orthodoxy of any political-economic period champions the interests of the dominant political group. Over the course of the FIRE Economy, economists working for institutions aligned with the government under both Republican and Democratic administrations agreed on key principles, such as the need for low inflation and interest rates, financial market deregulation, and a shift in the tax burden from property income to wage income, that aligned with the economic interests of the main beneficiaries of the FIRE Economy: the banks, financial institutions, and insurance and real estate companies. To those we can add health care and education, which have become financialized since 1980; households became unable to afford health care without insurance or education without borrowing, and credit inflated the costs of both in the way credit inflated home prices over the period.

The FIRE Economy captured economists as it did politicians, as well as many in the U.S. media, who with their bullhorns pitched tirelessly for FIRE products, primarily stocks and houses, and against health care divorced from the insurance industry. FIRE industry lobbies and political action committees backed the elections of public representatives, whether they wanted the backing or not, ensuring a continuation of policies to allow FIRE interests to grow richer and stronger. Data on the links between national campaign contributions by company and industry are available from nonpartisan Web sites such as opensecrets.org and on a state level at followthemoney.org.

Third, the impact of high oil prices on an economy are well understood, but the end of the dollar cartel and the disruptive dynamics of peak cheap oil forge new theoretical ground. There is no established economic theory for economists to use to model the potential impact of permanently rising oil prices. What limited theory does exist contradicts the establishment monetarist quantity theory of money that laid the foundation of the FIRE Economy with policies to control goods and services inflation—and, moreover, wage rates—while inflating asset prices. This theory worked for decades—until it didn't. In 2008 it all fell apart. Now a new economics is needed that builds on the thinking of the classical economists, takes the best from neoclassical thought, and adds an understanding of the proper and constructive role of finance in a newly productive economy. Where will this new economics come from?

IS APOLITICAL ECONOMICS POSSIBLE?

Economists like to think of their work as a social science. The neoclassicists, with their emphasis on equations and numerology, tried to make economics entirely mechanical, as if the forces moving the supply and demand curves were anything other than the results of decisions of groups of human beings who were influenced by their prejudices, circumstances, hopes and dreams, and the political environment of their day. The classical economists who came before them acknowledged that politics and economics are inseparable and so studied the political economy. Going forward, economics will return to that more honest tradition.

As a measure of just how political economics can be, consider the two most seemingly mundane and uncontroversial measures of economic health: unemployment and inflation.

To a layperson, the meaning of these two terms appears straightforward. Someone who is "unemployed" is qualified for a job but does not have one. A hundred years ago that is more or less how the unemployed were counted. But after the Great Depression, politicians took on a greater responsibility for providing jobs for voters. The measure of their success at this self-appointed task was the unemployment rate, determined by government institutions, such as the Department of Labor in the United States, as well as by "independent" groups. Once politicians both took responsibility for the unemployment rate and started calculating it, counting the unemployed was never the same.

The official definition of unemployed and the way unemployment is measured and reported in the United States changed frequently during the political administrations that oversaw the FIRE Economy. For example, before the Clinton administration, a worker who had been out of work for six months or more but had given up looking for work, and so became a "discouraged worker" by definition, was counted as unemployed in the standard measure of unemployment that you read in the newspaper, called U3 by the Bureau of Labor Statistics. During the Clinton administration the definition of unemployed was changed: It no longer counted discouraged workers. By the end of 2009, the officially reported unemployment rate was around 10 percent. However, if the same measures and definitions were used as in the 1980s' recession, the unemployment rate exceeded 17 percent. The unemployment rate is the ultimate barometer of economic policy. Which number conveys a worse policy outcome, 10 percent or 17 percent? It's not hard to see where the motivation to change definitions comes from. Proving political influence over economic statistics is problematic, but it is difficult to find an instance of data collection and reporting methods changing in ways that make an existing administration look worse.

Inflation and, more important, how to measure it, causes politicians to attempt similar contortions. What causes it? How to measure it? How to lower it when it is "too high"? How to raise it when it is "too low"? How much inflation, if any, is "good"? Who benefits and who suffers from it? What exactly is it? The answers to these questions are more politics than science. For the great inflation of the transitional economy, the story is especially vexing due to competing interpretations of the events leading up to it. Let's see if we can sort it out.

Devalue a currency and a wave of cost-push inflation surges through an economy without the central bank expanding the money supply. A weaker currency means that more units of that currency are needed to buy the same number of units of imported goods. Import prices rise. The higher import prices create price competition with domestically produced goods.

The FDR administration engineered such inflation in 1933 with a radical 70 percent devaluation of the dollar against gold to halt a three-year deflation spiral. The Nixon administration devalued the dollar twice in the early 1970s, shortly after promising never to do so. Between 2002 and 2008, the inflationary effect of a weak dollar was far larger than in the early 1970s, when the United States imported far less oil. America's number one import by dollar volume, oil is an input cost to nearly every good and service in an economy.

Food is, for all practical purposes, made out of oil. Oil is a key component of fertilizer, and food doesn't walk to your local grocery store; it's carried there on trains and in trucks that burn fossil fuels. In fact, it's hard to think of a single good or service that does not directly or indirectly depend on oil to exist, and if supply depends on oil, you can bet prices do too. As costs rise, if you are selling candy bars you either raise the price to customers or go out of business as the cost of inputs—milk, cocoa, and so on—rise to exceed your revenue. If you are selling haircuts, you have to raise the price to meet the cost of heating your hair salon, and of cosmetics and other supplies that are squeezing your profits.

Modern monetary systems are based on a combination of government credit-based money—called "fiat" money because it is created by the government by fiat—and private credit market money created whenever a consumer or business takes out a loan. The institutions that regulate the system, central banks, have a love-hate relationship with inflation. Too much inflation and a credit-based money system breaks down as interest rates rise. Too little and cascading defaults can tip the economy into debt-deflation. Deflation in the United States is not a risk, and in my opinion never was because of tools available to the Fed and a clearly stated intention to use them. The argument over whether inflation or deflation was likely to result from the credit bubble that peaked in 2007 ended when the Fed halted debt-deflation in March 2009. The only remaining risk is inflation. But what kind of inflation?

When inflation rises, the bond market demands higher interest rates as compensation for the risk of future losses to the purchasing power of the money that the borrower uses to repay the debt. They do this by refusing to buy bonds until the seller offers an interest rate that the buyer feels will protect them from future inflation. If a bond seller is offering a rate of 5 percent over ten years, but the market of bond buyers expects inflation to average 6 percent over that period, the bond will not sell; the seller must raise the rate to the level that the bond buyers demand—over the rate of expected inflation. The other factor determining interest rates is the bond buyer's assessment of default risk, whether the bond seller will at some point fail to make interest and principal payments on a bond. Markets set interest rates through this continuous auction among buyers and sellers as they come to an agreement on a price that reflects perceived default and inflation risks to set the prices of bonds as determined by the interest rate.

Inflation is one of the most confused and politically loaded topics in economics, second only to unemployment. Inflation is only meaningful to us as consumers as a measure of the quantity and quality of the goods and services we can buy with our income and savings.

Governments collect, analyze, and report on prices. In the United States, the Bureau of Labor Statistics of the Department of Labor collects inflation data on consumer and producer prices and issues consumer price index (CPI) and producer price index (PPI) reports monthly. For example, you might read in the paper that the CPI increased at a 3 percent annual rate in a given month. What do these numbers mean?

When inflation is high, governments tend to underreport it, for two reasons: one, because high inflation reflects poorly on monetary policy; and two, because interest rates on government bonds tend to reflect the reported rate of inflation; the higher the inflation rate goes, the more that government borrowing costs rise. Governments manipulate inflation statistics by changing the mix of items that they measure and by removing "volatile" items, such as energy and food, completely. The argument that the government gives for this practice of removing volatile (read: high) prices from the CPI is that rapidly changing prices complicate monetary policy and are not meaningful, because they are likely to fall as quickly as they went up, so there is no point in the government attempting to respond to these spikes with policy adjustments.

First of all, the practice of removing volatile components from an index is not statistically honest. Statisticians use a method called a "rolling average" to smooth volatile data in a series rather than remove it. Also, in the chart later in this chapter you can see that energy prices have been rising steadily since 2004; long-term volatility is an oxymoron.

Removing energy and food prices from inflation indexes has the effect of lowering the reported rate of inflation. To give you a sense of how much, the producer price index of finished goods without food and energy included peaked at around 4.5 percent in 2008, before the acute phase of the recession began. At the same time, the producer price index of finished goods including food and energy peaked at 10 percent. The PPI of crude energy materials alone rose an astonishing 80 percent year over year. One argument for including this data in the reported CPI is that doing so will increase public trust in the government; as anyone who purchased gasoline or food at the time was keenly aware, the reported peak CPI inflation rate of 5.5 percent was simply not credible.

A Web site called ShadowStats, created by John Williams, offers alternative inflation statistics for businesses. The theory behind the site is that key economic statistics, such as inflation and unemployment, have been modified so many times by the government over the past thirty years that today's CPI is nothing like the CPI of thirty years ago.

In truth, inflation as measured by the CPI is meaningless and a red herring. Other countries tend to rely more on an index of "personal consumption expenditures," or PCE price index. PCE measures total consumer spending by the type of item purchased. By measuring how much consumers actually spend versus how much items cost, PCE more accurately accounts for the decisions that consumers make over time to buy more of one kind of item or service than another. But PCE still does not take into account the fact that inflation affects different groups in society in different ways, a fact that takes on grave political importance given the hangover of income, wealth, and debt inequality from the FIRE Economy era and the inflationary forces that both peak cheap oil and the end of the dollar cartel will impose on U.S. households.

A socially meaningful measure of inflation takes account of the costs of all of the items and services that households actually buy. The question the inflation measure needs to answer is, Are the economic and monetary policies having an intended and desirable outcome for the majority of American citizens? To achieve that, we need an inflation index that measures the costs of household items as a percent of income across income groups, a measure of purchasing power of income. That is the true measure of sound policy.

We experience inflation as a mix of prices—of houses, autos, food, clothing, appliances, and so on—rising or falling against income. To see how, let's go to the case of a hypothetical median income earning couple we'll call Jack and Laura. Jack and Laura review the costs of other items they purchased when they first bought their home in 1965 to get an idea of the price of their home at the time they bought it compared to when they sold it thirty years later.

The Morris County Library of Morris County, New Jersey, maintains a historical record of prices advertised in the town's daily newspaper, the *Daily Record*. The paper has conducted the survey of advertisements over the first fifteen days of selected months every decade since 1900. The survey provides a unique look into how price changes affect daily life and living standards in America. The impact of inflation on living standards over time can be measured by observing how far prices rise or fall relative to income. We can see which goods consume more or less of the wages we earn, how much utility we get from these items, and how new products change the way we live.

The *Daily Record* survey includes staples, that is, items we buy frequently because we use them up. These include food, beverages, tobacco, alcohol, newspapers, and personal care and health items. We buy high-cost durable goods, such as automobiles and real estate, rarely. We buy durable goods seasonally, such as clothing, household goods, and recreational items. Special categories include garden equipment, school supplies, tools, and professional services such as lawyers. The authors made an effort to select items and brands, such as Kellogg's Corn Flakes, that are still found in today's stores, to help keep the comparisons accurate. This unique survey record makes it possible to take a "shopping list" all the way from 1900 and compare their retail prices today, at least for those items that you can still buy.

While the Morris County *Daily Record* survey data goes all the way back to 1900, for our purposes we will start by looking at a sample of survey prices when Jack and Laura Median bought their home in the early 1960s (see Figure 1).

The table shows the costs of various items as a percentage or multiple of income in three main categories: those that cost more of income in 2008 than in 1962; those that cost less; and those that cost about the same. At the end we add a few items that did not exist in 1962 but do exist today.

Starting with items that have increased the most as a portion of income, one stands out immediately: housing. A two-bedroom home costs more than three times as much of income in 2008 than in 1965. As is the case today, most homebuyers then purchased on a thirty-year fixed mortgage. In 1965, the interest rate was around 5 percent, lower than in 2008 but close enough that the cost of the mortgage is more or less the same now as then.

What happened to houses to justify a three-fold price increase?

FIGURE 1
Comparison of Prices to Median Income: 1962 versus 2008

Items that cost more	How many times or percent more does it cost now?	2008 Price ($)	1962 Equivalent ($)
Home, 2 bedroom	3.2	369,000.00	115,412.00
Home, 4 bedroom	2.7	675,000.00	250,722.00
Apartment, 3 rooms	2.6	1,775.00	677.00
Apples, McIntosh, per lb.	1.9	1.99	1.03
Lawn mower, 19"	1.84	729.00	397.00
Oranges, Valencia	77%	0.99	0.76
Sneakers	72%	50.00	35.91
Used mid-price car, 6 years old	41%	8,000.00	3,304.00
Hershey bar	36%	0.59	0.38
Bread	32%	1.69	0.54
Used mid-price car, 2 years old	30%	19,995.00	6,066.00
High-end car, new	18%	25,705.00	4,652.00
Mayonnaise	11%	4.40	0.50
Low-end car, new	10%	14,090.00	1,395.00
First class postage	10%	0.44	0.40
Items that cost less	**How many times or percent less does it cost now?**	**2008 Price ($)**	**1962 Equivalent ($)**
Women's casual dress	4.76	10.00	47.60
Television, high-end	3.68	2,700.00	9,949.00
Dishwasher	3.19	349.00	1,114.00
Washing machine	2.99	500.00	1,496.00
Camera (35 MM vs 10-megapixel digital)	2.67	399.00	1,067.00
Toothpaste	2.64	2.50	6.61
Hamburger (McDonald's)	2.5	0.89	2.23
Onions, 1 lb.	2.41	0.33	0.80
Shampoo	2.41	0.47	1.14
Beef, rib steak	1.58	3.99	6.29
Toothbrush	1.57	3.49	5.49
Eggs, dozen	1.55	2.29	3.54
Living room set (3-piece vs. 5-piece)	1.49	798.00	1,189.00
Men's casual slacks	1.32	30.00	39.56
Items that cost the same			
Gasoline	1%		
Broccoli	0%		
Butter	0%		
Did not exist in 1962	**Percent of monthly median income**		
Personal computer	12%		
Xbox	7%		
iPod	4%		
DVD player	2%		
Microwave oven	1%		

Does a home provide homeowners three times as much value relative to the value of the wages they earn to pay for it?

There are two factors that account for the difference: one, credit inflation produced by FIRE Economy tax and monetary policy intentionally designed to inflate the price of residential real estate; two, in the late 1980s home builders figured out that a large house is only marginally more expensive to build than a smaller house, but home buyers are willing to pay a lot more for a large one. Auto manufacturers learned this trick back in the 1960s. If you think about it, home prices should not have increased any more than the price of any other domestically produced item that is not subject to the deflationary forces of foreign trade and the benefits of the dollar cartel.

The prices of goods that the United States trades with the world have declined during the FIRE Economy era. Appliances and clothing are a markedly smaller part of personal expenditures than in 1965. This is consistent with the prices of items advertised in the *Morris County Daily Record* compared to incomes. Price competition between items made with U.S. versus foreign labor, which has been deflated by a strong dollar, not only makes these items less expensive to U.S. buyers but has also pushed down the price of similar products competing in the United States. If manufacturers in the United States cannot find labor that is able to work for wages that are low enough to allow them to offer the goods at competitive prices, the entire industry virtually disappears. This occurred in the textile industry starting in the 1980s and has been occurring in the high-tech manufacturing industry since 2001. A number of service industries, such as law, are also vulnerable unless the rules of the game change. The cost of housing must decline to allow Americans to live better with less income.

The difference between traded and nontraded goods and services explains other peculiarities in the *Morris County Daily Record* prices. Why are some food items, such as onions and eggs, nearly half as expensive today? The answer again comes down to a combination of factors, including technologies that deliver economies of scale and the purchasing power of the U.S. dollar relative to the currency of the trade partner that is selling its producer's goods to U.S. consumers. Onions are cheaper due to intense competition between U.S. and foreign producers whose currencies are either as strong as or weaker than the dollar. Eggs are now mass-produced, rather than grown in small, labor-intensive farms. One can argue that eggs are not as nutritious as they were in 1965, but they consume far less of income.

Autos are more expensive today relative to income, but only marginally so, from 18 percent more for a high-end car to 10 percent more for a low-end car. But unlike houses, autos have vastly improved in functionality and quality. They last far longer and require much less maintenance. Weighed against the value of their technological improvements, car prices are miraculous. This is an important point to drill down into to understand the workings of the TECI Economy.

Think of the price-to-value changes of technology-intense products such as autos this way. Imagine being able to drive a 2008 Ford Mustang back in time, in 1965, the year after the first Mustang rolled off the line. Say you pull up in front of the Ford Motor company headquarters in Dearborn, Michigan, and ask employees walking outside what they think of it.

Even before they enter the car or open the hood, they will have difficulty comprehending the paint and surface treatments under it that keep the sheet metal from rusting. The radial tires that last tens of thousands of miles and very rarely go flat. The LED taillights on curved acrylic that wrap around the back of the car and last longer than the car itself. The brilliant white halogen headlights that shine bright even in the midday sun. The tough yet flexible plastic that covers the bumpers. Never mind the shape of the car itself, impossible with methods of pressing steel available at the time.

Assume you can get them past the exterior before they call the Department of Defense to send someone down to find out what kind of devious criminal you are. As one of them runs into the Ford headquarters building to call the cops—there are no cell phones, of course— you pull an adventuresome employee inside and start to explain the automatic breaking and computer-controlled fuel-injection systems.

Long before you get to explaining the geopositioning satellite system that gives you directions on an LCD screen—a what?—and the voice-activated cell phone—a what phone?—and the entertainment system that plays MP3 files that you downloaded off the Internet—the what that you did what to from what?—the police arrive to take away the oddly dressed person who speaks English but keeps using these most peculiar words.

Another way to measure how much an item has increased in value—to separate out the inflation factors from others—is to ask how much Ford would have had to spend to reproduce a single 2009 car in the year 1965 with even a fraction of the features that are available in the lowest end car today?

First of all, the computers that control the braking, ignition, and other systems would need to be replicated in analog versus digital circuits. The integrated circuit (IC) first became commercially available in 1961. They were so expensive that only the military could afford to buy them. The Air Force, for example, used Texas Instruments's first ICs in their computers and the Minuteman missile in 1962. The original IC, the size of an adult's pinkie finger, sported one transistor, three resistors, and a capacitor. Today a dime-sized IC, the kind used in autos, holds 150 million transistors. In reality, there is no way Ford could in 1965 replicate the features of a 2009 Mustang at any price. The controls would be as big as the car itself. Putting aside that limitation, a round number guess at the cost is $10 million in 1965 dollars.

If you look at it that way, a $21,000 2010 Ford Mustang is a bargain compared to a $2,600 Ford Galaxy in 1965. If you hear someone tell you that a car costs ten times more today than forty years ago, and uses this fact as evidence that the currency has depreciated by a factor of ten, you can tell them that, compared to income, a car costs about the same, but in replacement value is worth five thousand times more.

Technology vastly increases the utility of autos. But the costs of owning a car grew above and beyond the sticker price for reasons that have nothing to do with technology and auto companies and everything to do with insurance companies and banks. We'll get back to houses shortly, which for obvious reasons cannot increase in utility the way cars have.

In 1965, the majority of auto buyers purchased cars with cash from savings. If they did borrow, a typical auto loan term was two years. At a 5 percent rate that increased the total cost of a car by approximately 10 percent. Today fewer than 10 percent of cars are purchased with cash, the average loan is four years, and interest rates average 8 percent, increasing the total cost of a car by a full third. Who gets the money? The financing arm of the auto manufacturer.

Auto manufacturers got into the financing business in the 1920s, but not until the FIRE Economy era did financing become their chief source of profits. In an intensely competitive global market, competing on features was tough; they found it easier to make money on service contracts and the financing, especially as their cost of borrowing declined but consumers' costs did not.

Getting back to our mix of household items and how the prices changed relative to income, energy has remained remarkably constant, with the exception of the period of the oil embargo in the late 1970s. As the FIRE Economy devolves, and the dollar gradually loses its role as the world's sole currency, more countries will trade with oil producers in local currencies. China will buy oil from Russia and copper from Peru in yuan instead of dollars. As global demand for dollars falls, the dollar price of oil will rise, and a long-standing relationship between energy prices and incomes in the United States will end. In fact, as you can see in the table on page 116, it began to in 2001, when the FIRE Economy started to dissolve.

Consumer electronics, appliances, clothing, and furniture are vastly less expensive, but this is due to a combination of cheap labor in goods-exporting countries and an overvalued dollar; both are coming to an end. Technology will keep pushing prices down, but only for those items that technology can improve. Which brings us full circle back to housing, and our median home buyers, Jack and Laura.

Why is a home purchase commonly considered an "investment" when home prices appreciate at a rate three times faster than incomes?

The nominal amount of $118,000 sounds like a lot more than $20,000, just as $2.5 million sounds like a lot of money today. But the purchasing power of Jack and Laura's income declined since 1965 against some goods and services but increased in others. The one area where the purchasing power of income fell dramatically is housing, where the same income buys one third as much housing value as before. This dramatic loss is due to FIRE Economy monetary and tax policy inflating the prices of homes far more quickly than wages and salaries.

The nominal amount of $118,000 sounds like a lot more than $20,000, just as $2.5 million sounds like a lot of money today. But the purchasing power of Jack and Laura's income declined since 1965 against some goods and services but increased in others. The one area where the purchasing power of income fell dramatically is housing, where the same income buys one third as much housing value as before. This dramatic loss is due to FIRE Economy monetary and tax policy inflating the prices of homes far more quickly than wages and salaries.

For nations suffering the trauma of high inflation, called "hyperinflation" if inflation rates exceed 100 percent in a year (as Argentina experienced most recently, starting in 2001), credit disappears almost entirely from the economy, and most transactions are done in cash. There is no price that a bond seller can offer a potential buyer to satisfy his or her fear that the bond will either be defaulted on or fail to pay interest at a rate higher than the rate of inflation. In either case, the bond buyer will lose money. Without a bond market, there is no credit market. But how does a nation get into such a mess?

If a nation's households are collectively overindebted, economic contraction can lead to debt deflation, and debt deflation can devolve into a general price deflation spiral. This happened in the United States in the 1930s. Households in the United States were overindebted as consumer credit borrowers when the great crash led into Great Depression, and were again as mortgage and consumer borrowers two generations later, before the great crash of 2008. Since the Great Depression, governments have come to view deflationary depressions as political kryptonite. Vast numbers of business failures cause high unemployment, which produces an army of angry voters. Turnover of political leadership follows recession as certainly as winter follows fall. Politicians pressure monetary authorities and their allies to make fiscal decisions to favor inflation—low interest rates and high levels of government spending—over more responsible policies, at least on their watch.

But the broad-based social injury of a deflationary depression can lead to revolutionary change in systems of government, such as from oligarchy to dictatorship, as millions of members of the middle class join the ranks of the poor, and the poor become destitute and angry. Politicians seek to avert deflationary depressions at any price, even if that price is the risk of high inflation in the future.

With all of this pressure from politicians, it's highly unlikely that any kind of nonpolitical economics is possible.

The unspoken truth: The FIRE Economy had left the nation wallowing in debt. After the collapse of the FIRE Economy, which had crowded out and financialized the productive economy for decades, the remnants of the productive economy fell with it, as the purchasing power of credit was withdrawn from households and businesses. In a cruel twist, the FIRE Economy left households overindebted and lacking savings to weather the rainy day that the FIRE Economy crisis visited upon the productive economy.

But the production economy hasn't gone away, because entrepreneurs haven't gone away. And entrepreneurial know-how provides the seeds of the TECI Economy—the future of the U.S. economy. First thing, the government has to get out of the business of propping up dying industries, and it has to stop throwing money into pork-barrel "shovel-ready" projects that only minimally improve our aging infrastructure. The real future of the U.S. economy is in turning back to making stuff again, smart technology to substitute for the financial engineering that brought us to our knees: clean, renewable energy to replace oil; and communications that will allow us to work together more productively. It's a bright future, and I'm hopeful for it. Chapter 4 describes it in more detail.

PART II
—
TECI

CHAPTER 4

—

THE TECI ECONOMY: TRANSPORTATION, ENERGY, COMMUNICATION, AND INFRASTRUCTURE

If there is a country in the world where concord, according to common calculation, would be least expected, it is America. Made up as it is of people from different nations, accustomed to different forms and habits of government, speaking different languages, and more different in their modes of worship, it would appear that the union of such a people was impracticable; but by the simple operation of constructing government on the principles of society and the rights of man, every difficulty retires, and all the parts are brought into cordial unison. There the poor are not oppressed, the rich are not privileged. Industry is not mortified by the splendid extravagance of a court rioting at its expense. Their taxes are few, because their government is just: and as there is nothing to render them wretched, there is nothing to engender riots and tumults.

—THOMAS PAINE, *RIGHTS OF MAN,* 1791

The original source of the great power of the United States is the inventiveness, resilience, and doggedness of its great people to nurture and strengthen the heart of its productive neoindustrial econ-

—

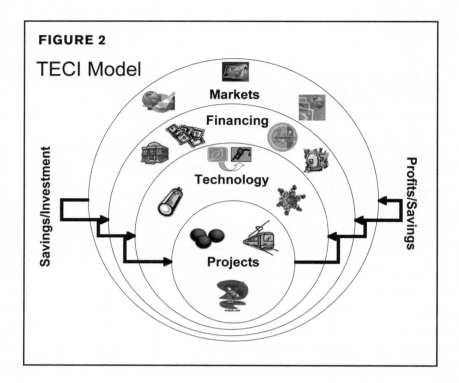

FIGURE 2

TECI Model

omy, which has now grown weak from decades of depletion by the nonproductive financed-based economy. Our decades of relying on the FIRE Economy have obscured this simple truth. And it provides the basis for the rise of a productive economy based on technology, energy, and a communication infrastructure—TECI.

The TECI Economy restarts the U.S. economy with stimuli produced by simultaneous cuts in the two major drags on the U.S. economy: the debt load left over from the FIRE Economy and the high energy intensity left over from the cheap oil produced by the dollar cartel. It also accounts for the lack of infrastructure investment over the thirty years when the FIRE Economy consumed households' and businesses' cash flows in the form of interest payments to banks instead of to taxes to pay for infrastructure. The TECI Economy cuts this debt burden even as it cuts our energy costs. In the American tradition, TECI also makes money in the process, by leveraging U.S. innovation capacity.

The FIRE Economy ran on public and private borrowing and consumption—on a continuous expansion of debt by businesses, households, and government. We're currently living through the transitional economy that resulted from the collapse of the FIRE Economy, as the lower purchasing power of credit and incomes force households to reduce consumption and FIRE Economy interests continue to influence government policy in an attempt to reinflate the prices of assets such as homes and commercial real estate rather than reduce the excessive debt built up during the FIRE Economy by writing off the principal to pre–credit bubble levels.

To grow the economy without continuous private sector debt growth, to build an economy based on saving and investment versus borrowing and consumption we need a solid economic foundation to build on. That foundation is the TECI Economy, which will allow the United States to face its challenge to compete in the world for investment capital and savings without the exorbitant privilege of the dollar cartel, a 0 percent savings rate, and debt that expands at a rate far faster than GDP.

The savings- and investment-based TECI economy will operate on a more even footing with other countries. The TECI Economy will shift the focus of economic policy away from continuous asset price inflation and onto rebuilding a modern and competitive productive economy.

WHAT TECI IS

The TECI Economy looks something like the productive economy of yore, in that it is built on investment in real goods. The difference is that the old productive economy focused on the manufacture of Industrial Age products and broke down when the United States began to invest in the FIRE Economy in response to foreign competition for those goods. As industry began to gain traction around the rest of the world—a process that continues even now—the United States simply couldn't compete; its labor costs were too high. If that's the case, why recommend the reindustrialization of America? Isn't that inviting disaster?

The "I" in TECI—infrastructure—is key.

REINDUSTRIALIZATION

Building the TECI Economy demands that the United States develop the productive industries it already has, definancialize them, and expand them to produce a range of solutions to the technical challenges that TECI projects will present.

Reindustrialization does not mean that the United States should revert to twentieth-century manufacturing. In the TECI Economy production takes on an expansive meaning; it includes any activity that produces a profit from adding value to tangible or intangible goods, as opposed to earning interest on debt or capital gains from asset price inflation. The core of the TECI Economy is massive projects that will make the United States once again the most entrepreneur-friendly country on Earth. This will involve reducing costs for private enterprise with tax cuts and reducing transportation, energy, and communications costs. The projects will be determined by business, not by government, and executed by public-private partnerships that compete for them and are rewarded for proper executions with high stock prices in the public market or punished with low prices for not meeting deadlines, quality, or design specifications.

Finance will continue to play an important role in the TECI Economy but will no longer *be* the economy. Consumer borrowing will continue, but only to finance appreciating assets, such as land and, after it has finished its postbubble decline, residential and commercial real estate. But the era of central banks–guaranteed borrowing, leveraging, and speculating—is over.

The primary short-term goals of these projects are employment and economic stimuli through a reduction in energy costs and the creation of demand for technological innovation that engages the U.S. technology start-up and financing industries. Longer term, the goals of TECI include the reduction of U.S. dependence on imported energy and the reduction of the energy intensity of the U.S. economy, both to lower energy overhead and to reduce foreign energy dependence.

To maximize the efficient use of limited capital, these projects are undertaken by public-private partnerships, hybrid government and private firms that can undertake high-risk, capital-intensive projects in an open and competitive bidding and execution model that reduces the possibility that projects devolve into insider privatizations.

The TECI Economy maximizes the use of private industry and markets and is built on three types of corporate and financing entities: capital intensive TECI projects called TECI P3; TECI technology innovator feeders that are usually technology start-ups but may be research groups within larger companies; and TECI funders that include the federal government, sovereign wealth funds (SWF), private equity and venture capital companies, and public markets.

The three main areas for competitive TECI P3s are: private-public partnerships in transportation (P3T), for projects such as high-speed rail; private-public partnerships in energy (P3E), for projects such as pebble bed nuclear reactors (PBNR); and private-public partnerships in communications (P3C), for projects such as fiber-optic cabling to private and commercial buildings.

Each project will have at least two but preferably three qualified global P3s bidding on it.

Each will in turn create demand for new technologies. New or existing energy technology start-ups will, for example, meet demand for new fuel-cell technology created by P3T transportation projects.

The TECI Economy, unlike the FIRE Economy, runs on equity, not debt financing. As a result, debt does not build up in the economy over time, and capital is efficiently recycled back into the economy to finance new projects. The primary source of economic growth for the TECI Economy is not interest on debt and capital gains from asset price inflation but profits from the sales of products and services.

The TECI Economy is not built out of thin air but by enhancing those parts of the U.S. economy that were either weakened by the FIRE Economy or that lay dormant during its rise. Journalists often claim that "America doesn't make or export anything," but they don't cite statistics. The fact is that the United States manufactures a great deal that the rest of the world wants and needs, and it is this unique productive capacity that we must nurture as the FIRE Economy winds down. The United States will rebuild on its ethics of hard work, education, fairness, and honesty; its culture of entrepreneurial versus financial risk taking, of competition, of saving, and of avoidance of debt; its core competencies in technology development and original invention; and its strong institutions of property rights and rule of law.

INTENSE ENERGY

Energy intensity is a key concept in understanding the necessity of the TECI economy. The term refers to the amount of energy needed to produce a dollar of GDP growth. As stated earlier, at the start of the FIRE Economy one dollar of new public and private sector debt was needed to generate a single dollar of GDP growth, but by 2007 five dollars of new debt were needed to produce a dollar of GDP growth. At the same time, the energy intensity of the U.S. economy declined 40 percent, from 15,450 BTUs used per dollar of GDP to 9,110. The good news is that more than half of this improvement came from increased energy efficiency. The bad news is that more than half came from the deindustrialization of the U.S. economy.

As U.S. economic output shifted away from energy-intensive industries, such as steel production, toward low-energy-demand FIRE and service industries, energy intensity declined. The challenge for the United States in a world where the cost of energy generally, and oil prices especially, is rising in dollar terms is to lower energy intensity while shifting toward a more production-based economy to increase economic output.

ENERGY EFFICIENCY

The TECI Economy is built on projects that reduce U.S. energy intensity by cutting the energy waste that accounts for more than 56 percent of our consumption, with the greatest gains to be made from transmission and transportation, which account for 26 percent and 21 percent respectively. We can cut electricity waste by more than half by generating it close to where it is consumed and by a combination of increased use of public transportation and the gradual replacement of the current fleet of commercial and personal transportation with lighter, although not smaller, hybrid automobiles running on liquid natural gas (LNG), diesel, and hydrogen fuel-cell cars. Energy-related technology demand will drive investment in new start-ups that reduce energy demand either via conservation or substitution.

ENERGY: THE BIG PICTURE

The scary-looking diagram on the following page is simpler than it appears to be at first. It represents in one graphic the whole flow of energy in a year in the U.S. economy.

There are two ways energy sources are consumed: They're either burned to generate electrical energy or burned directly in engines to move vehicles. The four main categories of users of energy are residential, commercial, industrial, and transportation.

The U.S. consumed 97 quads of energy in 2002. One quad is one quadrillion (1,000,000,000,000,000) BTUs, an amount of energy equal to 170 million barrels of oil. Six forms of energy used by the economy enter the chart from the left: nuclear, hydroelectric, biomass, natural gas, coal, and petroleum. Of those 97 quads consumed, 40 percent was as electricity. Of that electricity consumed, 8 percent came from nuclear generation, 6 percent from natural gas, and 20 percent from coal-powered plants. Electricity is used in fixed-energy applications, such as lighting and heating. The other 27 percent of U.S. energy not used for fixed applications is for transportation.

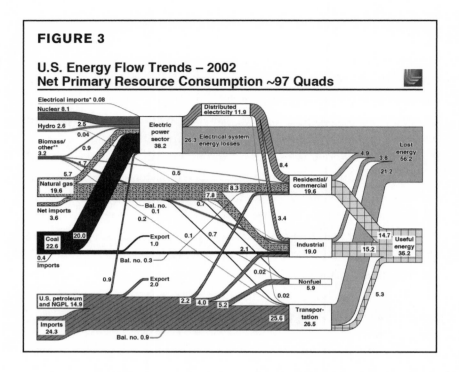

FIGURE 3

U.S. Energy Flow Trends – 2002
Net Primary Resource Consumption ~97 Quads

An astonishing 56 percent of all of the energy consumed is wasted. That means that less than half of the potential energy of the nuclear, gas, coal, and petroleum we use does useful work, such as moving cars, heating buildings, and smelting ore. Therein lies the largest opportunity for the TECI Economy, both in reducing the waste (and in the process the amount we need to use) and in driving new technology innovation that pays for itself in the form of energy cost cuts.

The most wasteful use of energy is transportation. Only 20 percent of the energy consumed actually moves people and products; the rest is wasted moving the vehicles that contain the people and products. The greatest savings can be achieved by reducing vehicle weight and by substituting commuting with telecommuting. A net decrease in transportation energy waste of 50 percent can reduce total energy waste by approximately 20 percent. The energy cost reduction to the economy is equivalent to a multitrillion-dollar tax cut over ten years.

Most of the natural gas and nearly all of the coal we use comes from inside the United States. Our single largest use of energy is transportation—planes, trains, and automobiles—followed by residential and commercial buildings, mostly in the form of lighting and heating, and industrial processes, such as smelting.

Of that 40 percent of our electricity energy use, a horrific 70 percent is wasted in transmission and other losses. This waste can be reduced by improving the efficiency of our power grid and by generating energy using smaller power plants that are located close to where the electricity is actually utilized. The model of a small number of gigantic power plants from which electricity is distributed by power lines over long distances made sense when fossil fuels were plentiful and the air they polluted appeared infinite. A wide range of energy products are needed that allow buildings to generate their own electricity, and use less too. In this chapter we'll look at some of the more promising electricity-generation technologies, such as pebble bed nuclear reactors—compact, modular, safe nuclear power plants—and energy savers such as LED lightbulbs that use as little as one tenth as much energy as a traditional incandescent bulb and last a thousand times longer.

CONSERVATION

The TECI Economy will run on far less energy than the FIRE Economy did, and even less than the transitional economy does. This will be accomplished by going after the low-hanging fruit of high energy intensity: waste. And although most of the waste is in transportation and energy transmission, there are also other, more subtle forms stemming from habit and culture.

Using less energy is not rocket science. Energy conservation can be achieved: in transportation, by reducing the mass of the vehicles; in electricity production, by not sending electricity over wires for long distances from centralized power-generation plants; and in buildings, by increasing insulation and moving away from lightbulbs that generate great heat with some light as a by-product. The solutions are not complicated, but they require the government to create the incentives for private industry to shift to a new, less wasteful energy paradigm. For example, before car manufacturers can build cars that run on liquified natural gas (LNG), LNG car owners need fueling stations as ubiquitous as gasoline stations. But in order for Gulf Oil, for example, to spend $300,000 per station to offer it, the company needs thousands of LNG cars on the road to see a return on investment. Government can end this market conundrum by financing the gas stations with cheap loans that Gulf can pay back over fifty years.

A considerable amount of transportation can be replaced by tele-commuting. Why is it necessary for millions of Americans to drive many miles to work in order to sit behind a computer when they could either stay home or drive a short distance to a facility nearby that is shared by a number of companies? In the TECI Economy, work from home and from shared office facilities will be the norm for any indus-try that does not involve physical product development, and even then, commuting every day will be the exception, not the rule. The idea of jumping on an airplane to visit customers will be replaced, at long last, with videoconferencing, in the fulfillment of a vision of video-based personal and business communications that started more than twenty years ago.

Not everyone can work from home, and not everyone who can work at home wants to. Suburban commercial office buildings left empty by the collapse of the commercial real estate market in 2009 will be resurrected by companies carving out space for employees who live nearby. The new generation of workers grew up using instant mes-saging and video to develop trust relationships without face-to-face communications. In the TECI Economy, face-to-face interaction will take on a new meaning, and be relegated to only the most important meetings.

The TECI Economy will be more energy-efficient, the efficiency achieved through the lack of funds businesses and households have to spend on heating, lighting, and transportation. Starting in 2008, the number of cars on the road in the United States declined for the first time since the end of World War II. That trend will continue for years, as Americans drive the cars they already have during the transitional economy. During this time the most energy efficient method of transportation on Earth, which delivers the lowest energy cost per passenger mile and is ubiquitous in all third world countries, will make a comeback in the United States—the bus. Long before high-speed rail and other major public transportation projects are developed and completed in the United States, a significant amount of travel that Americans previously did by car will be done by bus. As we've seen, the move to the bus will not be the only step down in living standards that Americans will make.

The development of a range of large but light cars powered by a range of fuels, primarily hydrogen and diesel, will also help drive the TECI Economy. The United States will have limited access to the higher grades of oil that are used to make gasoline, and new antipollution technology enables cars to run on diesel without producing more pollution than gasoline engines and yet are considerably more efficient, delivering sixty miles per gallon or more. Liquid hydrogen will be produced by new, small, and safe pebble bed nuclear energy plants located close to population centers where the energy is consumed, thus reducing electricity energy losses due to transmission (see page 137 for more on new nukes).

Another piece of low-hanging energy conservation fruit is the incandescent lightbulb. These bulbs are better described as efficient heaters that waste 10 percent of their energy as light. But they have one advantage: They are cheap to buy. Besides the fact that they use a lot of energy to produce not very much light, they burn out after a few hundred hours of use. Compact fluorescent bulbs are a reasonable bridge technology for lighting, but the ultimate answer is light-emitting diodes, or LEDs. Lights based on LED technology convert 80 percent or more of the energy they use into light and can last for ten years or more. In fact, LEDs used for military applications are rated for one hundred thousand years of continuous use, and for commercial applications can deliver similar performance characteristics.

This creates a number of exciting possibilities for architects. Most lighting fixtures are designed to allow access to lightbulbs that must be replaced. But what if the fixture is as permanent as the structure that it is placed in? Imagine lights built into concrete: Since the lights will last as long as the concrete itself, there is no reason to access them. Lights will be imbedded into the structures themselves. LEDs have quietly replaced incandescent lightbulbs in cars over the past ten years. Since they do not need to be accessed, because they will last as long or longer than the car they are in, automobile designers are freed up to create the sculpted look of modern car taillights.

For this reason alone, the TECI Economy world will look quite different than today's, because it will be lit by LEDs that free architects and designers to create lighting and buildings that cannot exist today. The result will be a dramatic change in the way the world looks, especially at night, when the lights go on.

ALTERNATIVE ENERGY

With abundant coal, gas, and uranium resources, the United States has plenty of fuel for fixed energy generation. Incentives to reduce carbon emissions are on the way, which will enable the rebirth of new, safer nuclear power plants in the United States based on a modern and more scalable and safe nuclear energy production model built by PPPs. If properly structured, these can combine the efficiency of the private sector and the unique ability of government to take on the gigantic financial risks that a large-scale nuclear build-out poses.

The primary energy challenge faced by the United States is fuel for transportation. Today the United States imports more than 62 percent of the oil it consumes. But rather than try to manufacture alternative new fuels such as bio-diesel, a process that requires energy, the United States will instead use less of those that nature made, such as diesel refined from petroleum; the alternatives will simply be too expensive.

At first, the transitional economy will create energy conservation discipline and changes in America's energy-use culture, because we simply will not be able to afford to use as much energy after peak cheap oil. The habit of jumping into a large pickup truck to fetch a pint of milk ten miles away will be replaced by one of planning shopping in advance to reduce the frequency of trips, as well as by the use of small vehicles for the task.

No one likes to feel that changes brought about by a loss of purchasing power and a corresponding reduction in living standards were imposed by forces beyond their control. Instead, these changes in habits of energy use will be embraced as a lifestyle choice, adopted like many others as Americans cope with declining living standards. Thrift will be the New Americanism, and clever consumer products companies will latch onto this need to turn a sense of loss of options into a positive choice and will market products to consumers using messages that emphasize the consumer's desire to be less wasteful, when in fact the opportunity to be wasteful has been vastly curtailed by a lack of income and credit.

New Nukes

Nuclear power will experience a resurgence in the TECI Economy because the economics favor generating electricity from a relatively inexpensive fuel that is plentiful in the United States and that generates a fraction of the greenhouse gasses of the alternative fuel, coal. While nuclear energy will reduce reliance on foreign energy supplies and help the United States stay within carbon cap limits, the United States has a troubled history to overcome with this technology.

The industry never recovered from the Three Mile Island disaster in 1980, and no nuclear reactors have been built in the United States for more than thirty years; the United States was able to fall back on an abundant supply of coal to meet its electricity needs. Today, only 20 percent of America's electricity is generated by a total of 140 nuclear power plants. Unfortunately, burning coal produces greenhouse gases.

Consider other countries where coal or natural gas alternatives to nuclear power generation are limited. In France, for instance, 59 nuclear power plants produce 89 percent of the country's electrical energy, or more than four times as much as in the United States. France was able to build so many reactors relative to the country's size by manufacturing essentially the same reactor over and over, rather than many one-off designs, as was attempted in the United States, as well as by streamlining the licensing and certification process.

The ultimate solution for the United States is to build a large number of small nuclear reactors near population centers where the electricity is consumed. That way, not only are greenhouse gas emissions reduced by substituting nuclear for coal and gas powered plants, but the 60 percent electricity energy waste from long-distance transmission can be reduced by half or more.

If a large number of small reactors are built, they'd better be safe. The answer to the safety issue is pebble bed nuclear reactors, or PBNR. Just as lighting in the future will be based primarily on LED technology, the nukes of the future will be PBNR.

On the surface, like most breakthrough technologies, the PBNR, one of several third-generation nuclear power plant designs, looks too good to be true. PBNRs have few moving parts; are meltdown-proof, and so do not need complex and expensive safety features or even a containment vessel surrounding the reactor; can be made in a modular Lego-blocks fashion from small enough to power a town to large enough to power a small city; and the fuel can be transported and recycled at low cost.

The beauty of the PBNR is simplicity. Rather than rods of fissile material that must be mechanically controlled to heat water, the fuel is in the form of spheres that heat gas. Imagine a giant gumball machine, and in it instead of gumballs are tennis ball–sized spheres of processed uranium encased in graphite, called "pebbles." Piled up inside a reactor vessel, the pebbles produce heat when the fissile material in one pebble reacts with the pebbles around it. The pebbles can never get too close to each other, so there is no chance of the kind of accident that can occur in liquid-cooled reactors when the mechanical controls fail and materials overheat and melt unless safety features prevent the meltdown. An inert gas enters the containment vessel, heats to around 1600 degrees Celsius as it is poured between the pebbles, and expands. The expanding gas runs turbines that power generators to produce electricity. Simple. PBNRs are the most efficient nuclear reactors, converting 50 percent of the energy contained in the fuel into usable electrical power.

Currently, PBNRs are new and only running in a prototype phase in China, but the U.S. Nuclear Regulatory Commission is PBNR-friendly and "gets" the fundamental advantages of the design.

That PBNRs can be built in a modular fashion permits their deployment at remote sites, where most of the manufacturing can be conducted at an off-site facility using assembly-line-like techniques to achieve economies of scale. This design allows them to be constructed in one-hundred-megawatt increments, so customers can tailor the sizes of potential plants to meet the particular needs of a project or geographical area—from a small town to a city. The fuel design—pebbles that rest on the bed of the reactor vessel—means that the temperature is far more predictable than in water-based reactors, making regulation easier. The near inability to cause a meltdown during even a severe accident means containment structures are technically unnecessary, which would greatly reduce costs, but PBNRs will be built with containment structures anyway to appease public concerns. By utilizing continuous refueling, PBNRs do not have the refueling requirements of light-water reactors, and do not even have to be shut down periodically for refueling as light-water reactors are. Because of their inherent safety, emergency planning zones surrounding PBNR plants can be much smaller than those for the equivalent light-water plant.

As compelling as these advantages are, the best feature of PBNRs is that, unlike light-water reactors, the "waste" heat is gas that is so hot that it can be used for hydrogen production. Imagine hundreds of small, safe PBNR nuclear power plants, which produce nearly zero greenhouse gas emissions, spread around the country generating liquid hydrogen that can be used to power vehicles that produce nearly zero greenhouse gas emissions.

NEW CARS

At the tail end of the FIRE era, as oil prices increased to $147 and gasoline to over $4 in a burst of cost-push inflation, innovative fuel-efficient cars made a brief comeback in the United States. But the inflation quickly ebbed when the recession started in 2008, and those innovative cars, such as gasoline hybrids, were hit especially hard due to their price premium and gasoline prices that plunged below $2.

Many two-car families will become one-car families, with the smaller of the two cars previously used favored while the second car sits unregistered and uninsured. During the TECI Economy, the old fleet of cars left over from the FIRE Economy era—the average more than ten years old—will begin to turn over. The forcing function for adoption will be the declining purchasing power of wages in the United States to buy fuel, meaning for the first time in generations Americans will work more hours to pay for transportation than in the past because the dollar will not purchase as much energy as before.

The new cars will not be exotic hydrogen fuel-cell cars but hybrids that burn diesel, the most abundant and cheaply available fuel in the United States. Here's a quick rundown of available technologies and why diesel hybrids will dominate.

Diesel

Diesel vehicles are associated with plumes of black smoke and smelly exhaust, but modern diesel engines and pollution-control equipment make that perception obsolete. Nearly every auto manufacturer will offer diesel cars and trucks for sale in the United States by 2012. With high fuel mileage typically in excess of fifty miles per gallon and new methods of cleaning up emissions, diesel is the fuel of the future.

Diesel engines alone are 30 percent to 35 percent more efficient than gasoline engines. Depending on the size of the vehicle, diesel cars and light trucks get around forty miles per gallon compared to an equivalent gasoline-powered automobile that gets twenty-five miles per gallon or a gasoline hybrid that gets forty-five miles per gallon. In fact, diesels qualify for income tax credits just as gasoline hybrids do. So why doesn't everyone drive a diesel?

In many European countries diesel autos are more numerous than gasoline ones. Heavy taxation of gasoline and diesel across Europe has over decades resulted in a cultural adjustment to the kind of high fuel prices that Americans will start to see as peak cheap oil arrives in waves over the next five to ten years. Europeans drive smaller cars, and more of them diesels, because they are more fuel-efficient. When peak cheap oil begins to drive up the prices of gasoline and diesel, the American drivers will trade in the gas-guzzling cars they have left over from the FIRE Economy era for smaller vehicles.

At the time of this writing, several pieces of legislation have been proposed to move this inevitable process forward at a time when the U.S. auto industry needs the boost. Automobile unit sales in 2009 fell below levels last experienced at the bottom of the early 1983 recession, when the U.S. economy was half as big. The 1983 recession was manufactured by the Federal Reserve in order to lower inflation by raising unemployment. The transitional economy, on the other hand, occurred despite every effort by monetary authorities to prevent it—interest rate cuts, tax cuts, and deficit spending programs.

In May 2009, Congress agreed to pass legislation to give consumers billions of dollars to trade in their old cars and trucks for models with higher gas mileage. The subsidy, popularly known as "cash for clunkers," was intended to increase U.S. vehicle sales, with special provisions to support the faltering American auto industry, and to make the nation's car and truck fleet more efficient. President Obama supported the idea, and money was put into the 2009 stimulus package to finance it. The program is widely considered unsuccessful at achieving either of its intended goals of boosting the U.S. auto industry and lowering the age of the auto fleet by replacing old cars and SUVs with more fuel efficient models. According to a *Chicago Tribune* story, Almost 700,000 new vehicles were purchased under the Cash for Clunkers program in late 2009. Before the program in mid-2009 auto unit sales had collapsed to 1983 levels. Sales increased briefly to levels first reached in 1985 during the program but fell back to 1983 levels after the program ended. The net result was to pull some auto sales from 2010 into 2009. The net impact on the auto fleet was equally uninspiring. The average age of America's cars and trucks fleet was ten years before the program and 9.8 years after, a 2 percent improvement. According to a report by the automotive Web site Edmunds.com, only 125,000 of the 700,000 vehicles sold would not have been sold anyway. With a total tab of $3 billion, the Cash for Clunkers stimulus program cost taxpayers $24,000 per car. The program did have a statistical benefit: it added 1.7 percentage points to the nation's forth quarter gross domestic product according to BLS statistics.

Until recently, diesel engines did not run cleanly enough to pass emissions requirements in U.S. states with high air quality standards. Diesel burns less cleanly than gasoline in internal combustion engines and requires more extensive antipollution equipment.

Hydrogen Fuel Cells

Cars that use fuel cells convert hydrogen fuel to electricity and emit only water as a by-product. Fuel cells are highly efficient, converting 80 percent of the energy capacity of the fuel into usable electricity. By comparison, internal combustion engines are only 25 percent to 30 percent efficient.

Highly efficient and clean fuel-cell vehicles appear to be ideal, but daunting challenges to affordability and their limited range have kept them off the market. The greatest limitation of hydrogen is range. After more than a decade of research and development, only the Honda FCX Clarity is commercially available; it has a 270-mile range per tank of hydrogen and delivers the equivalent of 68 miles per gallon, according to Honda. The energy density—the number of BTUs of energy by weight or volume—for hydrogen is comparable to gasoline by weight, but by volume hydrogen has less than one third of the energy density, and even accounting for the greater efficiency, it requires twice as much space. There is no way around this limitation.

Another limitation is that the hydrogen, unlike gasoline that is refined from oil, has to be manufactured from water. Hydrogen is not a fuel so much as it is a kind of liquid battery that stores energy in a form that can be converted into electricity in a fuel cell.

Pure Electric Vehicles

Pure electric vehicles, or EVs, have been pitched by focusing on two key advantages: zero tailpipe emissions and speed off the line. The first advantage is debatable, because the electrical power needed to charge the car's batteries had to be generated someplace, and in the United States that place is most likely to be a coal-fired or gas-fired power plant. The EV's carbon footprint is made many miles away. Worse, the sum of the inefficiencies of electricity generation, transmission, and battery charging make the electric no more energy-efficient than an internal combustion engine car. An EV that runs off a fuel cell—an onboard electric power plant that usually runs on hydrogen or methane—is far more efficient. But as mentioned before, lack of availability of fuel and low energy density make this solution unviable today.

A key performance difference between an electric motor and an internal combustion engine is that the latter reaches maximum torque when the engine is turning at a rate of thousands of revolutions per minute. This makes them relatively slow off the line even compared to a puny EV, because electric motors reach maximum torque at zero revolutions per minute. But the off-the-line advantage is a mixed blessing. Once a pure electric gets up to speed, torque drops off dramatically. This limitation is solved with a special transmission.

The pure electric car is the very first type of car ever made, back in the late 1800s. One reason they have never come into widespread use is lagging battery technology, but that is part of the problem. Pure electrics have three killer limitations today.

The worst limitation is that they cannot be used while they are being charged. To use an electric car you have to plan ahead, and drivers are not used to having to calculate whether they'll have enough juice to complete a trip. If you unexpectedly need to use a pure electric car and it is not charged, you're out of luck. It's not like running low on gas, when you can quickly fuel up and be back on the road. You will have to wait, usually for hours, before you can use the vehicle. That limitation is the primary reason pure electrics have languished for over a hundred years, and no amount of battery technology will fix it. The charge time can be shortened but never brought down to the five-minute recharge time of a car that burns diesel or gasoline. There are two solutions to this problem that will evolve over the next ten years.

A company called Better Place is developing one solution to the battery recharge time problem. The idea is to make modular, pre-charged batteries available at service stations. The EV driver pulls up to an automated system that exchanges the car's discharged batteries for new ones that are already charged. The whole process takes less time than that needed for refilling a fuel tank with gasoline or diesel.

While this sounds great in theory, as usual the devil's in the details. Battery replacement stations only solve the pure electric auto owner's problem if there are enough stations within a driver's range to keep the auto going for long trip. Until the driver is assured that there are Better Place battery replacement stations in the middle of Montana, a cross-country drive is out of the question, and so the auto's range is effectively limited to the area where recharging stations are available. This makes the Better Place model work better in smaller countries, such as Japan, or on islands, like Hawaii. Even so, government investment is necessary to overcome this chicken-and-egg problem: Pure electric manufacturers can't build vehicles in volume until the recharging stations are in place to overcome the consumer's objection to recharge wait times, and the service station owners, or Better Place itself, cannot make money on battery replacement services until there are enough pure electric autos on the road to create enough daily demand to make the stations economically viable.

A more promising approach to EV battery charging that does not require massive infrastructure investment and can evolve slowly along with the EV industry, but one that will take many years to develop, is based on the "top off" recharge model. The idea is that EV drivers, like laptop and mobile phone users, want to keep their EV's batteries mostly charged most of the time. They want to be able to top off their EV's batteries when they are shopping at the mall or at work by plugging into a simple recharge station wherever they park, ten minutes here, two hours there. A clever Boston start-up called inCharge, founded by Dror Oved, is developing a product to do this.

For this reason hybrids will continue to be the fuel efficient design of choice for consumers for the next decade.

Hybrids

The term "hybrid" refers to propulsion systems made up of a combination of an electric motor and a smaller than usual internal combustion engine. Fuel efficiency over a traditional internal combustion engine auto is gained by combining the power of both engines during acceleration and then the recapture of energy normally lost in braking; that braking energy is used to recharge the batteries that drive the electric motors. Some of the efficiency gains of an electric car are gained without the primary disadvantage of a pure electric car, that they cannot be used when they are being recharged.

The missing part needed to make hybrid and electric autos true breakthrough products is batteries that deliver high energy density, long life, and a fast charge, and that can be cheaply recycled and are safe and reliable. New technology developments show real, practical promise. For example, Boston Power, a lithium-ion or Li-ion battery technology company based in Westborough, Massachusetts, offers a promising next-generation battery for the hybrid and pure electric vehicle markets. I met with the company's brilliant and charismatic founder and CEO, Christina Lampe-Onnerud. She came to the United States from Sweden to get a postdoctorate from MIT and stayed to build a technology company and fulfill a dream. She, like many European entrepreneurs, is attracted to the opportunities that the United States presents to scientists to turn an invention into a commercial enterprise. With more than one hundred patents pending, her company aims to change the formula for transportation use worldwide.

Lithium-ion batteries are not new. They have been around since the 1970s and commercially viable since the early 1990s. But as is often the case with revolutionary changes in markets, a missing piece of the puzzle can enable a technologic leap forward that changes the playing field among entrenched players.

Boston Power is among a group of companies that seek to enable a potentially revolutionary change in vehicles and storage systems for home "on the grid" power generation. The fundamental challenge of wind and solar power generation is that wind power only produces energy when the wind is blowing and solar when the sun is shining. Backup power needs to be available to meet electricity demand when the wind and sun cannot, and that means building expensive backup coal- or natural gas–fired electricity generation plants. To go fully green and eliminate hydrocarbon based electricity generation plants from the equation, wind and solar need efficient, recyclable, dependable electricity storage. Boston Power's approach is a unique battery technology platform that is based on a flat, oval-shaped, prismatic cell design. These cells can be discharged and recharged many more times than conventional lithium-ion cells according to the company. They have built-in safety and reliability features that are critical for transportation and home applications.

Boston Power claims that its batteries deliver nearly twice the power density of cells used in hybrid and electric vehicles today. They can be recharged to more than a thousand times before performance begins to degrade. They charge to 80 percent capacity in only thirty minutes and to 40 percent capacity in ten minutes. They offer multiple redundant safety features.

Boston Power's battery technology promises to enable a whole new market of consumers who want to buy ultraefficient hybrids and pure electric cars. Millions of drivers who today spend five minutes to fill their car's gas tank to half full will accept the inconvenience of taking an extra five minutes to half fill their "electricity tank" if they know their next refill is as readily available as a common 120 volt plug. They will never "run out of gas" or have to wait hours to recharge.

The greatest challenge EV manufacturers face is battery cost. EV makers need batteries that offer more range due to higher energy density by weight and a longer life because they can be recharged many times without degrading. But even if better batteries appear, the EV market growth will continue to be gated for years by the limited availability of recharging stations. Rather than EVs, a combination of new battery technology and new lower emission, high efficiency diesel engines in diesel hybrids will leverage existing infrastructure and put America on the road to a low energy intensity transportation system.

A diesel hybrid is like a gasoline hybrid except that the already significant fuel efficiency of a diesel engine is added to the efficiency gains created by combining an internal combustion engine with an electric motor. Hybrid diesel is the vehicle power plant of the future, but there are several technical challenges to the parts of that whole solution that have to be overcome.

When the first diesel hybrids hit the market in 2010 with fuel mileage ratings of seventy-five miles per gallon, the next big trend in bringing down both the fuel inefficiency and emissions of the American passenger car fleet will have begun. Gradually, the FIRE Economy gas hogs will be replaced by hybrid electric and diesel-fueled trucks and autos.

Later, after the TECI Economy gets a footing, America regains its competitive standing in the world economy, and the infrastructure has evolved to support it, Americans can look forward to a whole new generation of hydrogen and LNG-powered electric and plug-in hybrid cars.

The ideal short-term solution to the transportation fuel efficiency part of the energy cost-cut equation that will get us to a 50 percent reduction in energy intensity in five years is plug-in diesel hybrid–powered vehicles.

The ideal long-term solution from the standpoint of both reducing U.S. dependence on petroleum and reducing costs and carbon emissions are hydrogen fuel cell–powered vehicles with hydrogen generated by a variety of methods, from pebble bed nuclear power plants to wind to solar, close to where it is consumed.

Boston Power is an ideal example of a reindustrialized America, a made-in-USA technology company that will enable a major cut in the energy intensity of the global economy by increasing the efficiency of vehicles, and thereby reducing net mobile- and fixed-energy demand. The batteries may be manufactured in China and other countries, where manufacturing labor is less expensive, but the profits from the sales will flow into the United States, where they accumulate as savings available to finance investment in new companies like Boston Power, creating a virtuous cycle of saving, investment, and job creation. The jobs created are high-paying positions in engineering, material science, and systems design, and in testing, marketing, and distribution.

GETTING TO TECI

Long term, the United States needs to grow its way out of debt and build a platform for a new era of competitive growth. In chapters 5 and 6, I address the midterm macro picture that stands between us and TECI, and what opportunities and challenges we'll face. With business and personal incomes down along with asset prices, tax revenues plunged by more than 30 percent in 2009 and will not recover until businesses start to hire again and unemployment starts to fall.

Without tax revenue, and unable to increase foreign borrowing, where will the U.S. government get the money to finance the projects that form the core of the TECI Economy?

There is really only one answer. We need the discipline and efficiency of the private sector combined with the legal backing of the federal government. To finance the reindustrialization of the U.S. economy, we need TECI Economy partnerships between government and private enterprise—public-private partnerships.

WHAT IS A PUBLIC-PRIVATE PARTNERSHIP?

As defined earlier, a public-private partnership is a joint business venture between private industry and government. The joint venture is financed and operated as a partnership of the local, state, or federal government with one or more private sector companies. Imagine a company that is part General Electric and part U.S. government.

Many varieties of PPP exist, but for our purposes we will focus on those that apply to the task at hand, building the TECI Economy. One PPP arrangement that applies is that the government uses tax revenue to provide capital for investment to finance the project. Once the project is completed, operations are run jointly with a private operator under contract. In another option that applies to next generation nuclear energy, called private finance initiatives, capital investment is made by the private sector on the guarantee of a contract with the government to provide agreed services. Alternatively, government contributions to a PPP may be in-kind from the transfer of existing assets. Government may provide a capital subsidy in the form of a one-time grant to attract private investors or support a project with revenue subsidies, such as tax breaks, or guarantee annual revenues for a fixed period.

The PPP is formed when a private sector consortium forms a special company called a "special purpose vehicle" or SPV to develop and operate a road, bridge, power plant or other asset for the contracted period. The process is not unlike a production company that forms to create a movie, except that after disbanding after the "product" is made, a portion of the company remains to maintain and operate the resulting product, such as a power plant. In cases in which the government has invested in the project, the government gets an equity share in the SPV. A consortium is usually made up of a building contractor, a maintenance company, and a bank. The SPV acts as the general contractor that signs up the government and subcontractors to build the asset and then maintain it. Any project that can guarantee and secure positive cash flows is a prime candidate for financing.

The Big Dig is the name that Boston locals gave the Central Artery/ Tunnel Project (CA/T) megaproject that rerouted the Central Artery (Interstate 93), the chief highway through the heart of Boston, into a 3.5-mile tunnel under the city. In 1985 the project was forecast to cost $2.8 billion, or $6 billion in 1982 dollars, but by its completion in December 2007 it cost over $14.6 billion. Including $7 billion in interest, the total cost is a staggering $22 billion, which will not be paid off until 2038. Besides the extreme cost overruns, the project suffered innumerable delays and instances of fraud that resulted in arrests and convictions. All in all, the Big Dig is a perfect example of government doing a terrible job at selecting and executing on a major public works project.

PPPs are government and private enterprise hybrid corporations. They are suitable to large-scale projects that incur such high risks to capital that no private corporation will attempt to build them. Statistically, on a global basis, PPPs turn in projects on time and under budget. The reason is simple: incentives. Often confused with the concept of privatization, which is to be avoided at all costs, PPPs offer a way for governments to make the most efficient use of limited capital resources. There are right ways and wrong ways to structure PPPs, but if the lessons are learned from several hundred years of experience of private development of public infrastructure, including in the early days of the United States, when highways were built by European firms with European investors' money, they offer a way for America to develop the TECI Economy without wasting precious national credit or taking on additional debt burdens.

The popularity of PPPs is cyclical. According to the Collaboratory for Research on Global Projects (CRGP), the popularity of PPPs for infrastructure provisioning runs in hundred-year cycles, evolving through various arrangements ranging from mostly government financed and operated to mostly privately financed and operated, starting with concession arrangements between private companies and government and finally to fully privately owned and operated projects.

First comes the building and operation of projects by government employees, for example, the U.S. highway system after World War II. The next model that is adopted is the outsourcing of the building of projects to private companies, while the subsequent operation of the resulting road is managed by a public entity. In this case there is no divestiture or leasing of public property by the government to private firms. The Big Dig in Boston is an example of this model. The model later evolves to both private development and operation of project, the build-own-operate model that is referred to as privatization. The UK followed this model with limited success during the 1980s and 1990s.

This progression from purely public to purely private infrastructure development follows from the wherewithal of government to finance needed infrastructure development and operations out of public funds. The tendency of governments over time to take on too much debt and accumulate excessive and unsustainable public liabilities, such as pensions and health care, has led many a government, such as the United States today, into a financial and fiscal bind, unable to pay for needed infrastructure development out of tax receipts or public borrowing alone. PPPs have been the favored approach to infrastructure development by states facing fiscal crises, such as Spain, the UK, and Chile. PPPs are also favored by new states that have limited domestic funds and skills, such as the United States in the 1800s, when European private financing built canals and roads, or that are growing fast and don't have a lot of time, such as China today.

The driving force of this evolutionary process is excessive debt. Governments accumulate debt over a period of decades when the economy is strong and financing both debt payments and infrastructure development and maintenance costs is feasible. One day the economy turns down and the government finds itself stuck with more debt and infrastructure costs than it can finance, but rather than restructure the excessive debt, it instead turns over the job to private companies in exchange for toll or other use revenue, or even sells off public assets to private companies if it gets desperate enough. It's time to acknowledge where the Unites States is in this cycle and rather than let it run its course, which can be economically destructive if it causes further concentration of wealth and power, get ahead of it and think through ways to structure companies and projects to avoid PPP pitfalls.

PPPs deliver on projects more efficiently than government, and the statistical evidence is strong that PPPs deliver projects under budget and on time. The arguments against them are: They are a form of privatization that gives public property to government insiders; public employees will lose jobs, though there is no net gain in employment; private profit motive will result in lower service levels; and projects are awarded to insiders. These are all valid concerns that need to be addressed in the structure of the PPPs themselves and in the way projects are awarded.

The CRGP recommends a new PPP model with three key elements that prevent the kinds of problems that typically develop with them: competition, risk transfer, and life-cycle perspective.

Competition is a tenet of the TECI Economy generally, along with open access, meaning any qualified and experienced firm from around the globe must be allowed to compete for a project. This increases efficiency, maximizes innovation, and taps into a global pool of best practices knowledge. The worst examples of PPPs that have evolved into some of the most egregious privatizations, such as in the UK, can be avoided if the risk remains with the private firms that manage a project, specifically cost, schedule, and service levels. PPPs must have full life-cycle cost liabilities in order to create the incentives to develop projects that are not only cost-efficient to build but also to operate and maintain.

The three most common criticisms of the PPP model are: The public loses control of public assets to private companies, the lack of competition between vendors for PPP projects means that costs benefits of competition are often not realized, and interest costs add unnecessarily to total costs. These criticisms are fair, but these problems are implementation issues, not problems inherent to the PPP model itself.

Loss of public control of public property to private companies is a valid concern, but it can be addressed in the structure of the PPP contracts themselves. The most simple and popular approach is for government to lease rather than sell the public property to a private entity, so that the public sector has ultimate control over the asset.

Competition for contracts is critical in order for the cost benefits of private development and ongoing maintenance of infrastructure to accrue. The fear is that sole bids on projects will result in high costs. While this can occur, in practice, more often than not, competition results in underbidding. The winning firm then later has to either ask for additional funds or abandon the project.

The concern that PPPs add to total costs is not supported by the data on successful programs. The first PPPs were developed in countries and cities that did not have access to debt financing to fund infrastructure projects. The United States can adopt the model more widely in order to avoid debt financing and the layering of economic rents on top of infrastructure development and maintenance costs. One approach that economist Michael Hudson has recommended is that a portion of the development cost be tied to property taxes on land and buildings that benefit from the infrastructure investment. As the property values of the adjoining land rises, so do the tax revenues that pay off the development costs and finance ongoing maintenance.

Thousands of PPP projects in a dozen countries over one hundred years provide plenty of examples of successful and unsuccessful examples to learn from. No solution is perfect, but the risks that widespread adoption of the PPP model presents are lower than the risks posed by not improving the nation's infrastructure to make the country more energy-efficient and competitive, or by attempting to finance projects with government debt and worsening the fiscal position of our local, state, and federal governments.

ESCAPE FROM DEBT: THE VENTURE CAPITAL FINANCING MODEL

If enemy number one in the climb out of economic recession, from the transitional economy to the TECI Economy, is the debt hangover from the FIRE Economy era, creating more debt is not going to solve the problem. Debt is the problem. How to finance public-private partnerships without creating even more debt? By using bonds that convert debt to equity. Besides not adding to the already excessive level of debt in the economy, financing projects with bonds that convert to equity from the beginning guarantees that profitability is built into the projects, and in fact protects against the development of wasteful projects that will not produce a return on investment.

Infrastructure convertible bonds (ICB) can be sold to U.S. investors directly by local, state, and federal governments much as individual and institutional investors can buy U.S. Treasury and savings bonds via the Treasury Department Web site. This eliminates the costs of middlemen, such as investment banks, further reducing costs. Once bonds convert to equity they begin to trade with the PPP's shares in the public markets.

What can the United States sell to foreign investors as the Treasury bonds and other U.S. debt, such as agency debt, mature? The central banks of China, Japan, and Russia can buy ICBs via sovereign wealth funds. This will reduce some of the pressure on the dollar from the sales of dollar-denominated debt as the world transitions away from a dollar-centric international monetary system.

HUMAN CAPITAL

The TECI Economy does not only rely on big projects and creative financing; it also demands the resurrection of American virtues of self-sufficiency and limited government.

One of the more unfortunate side effects of the FIRE Economy is that American culture adapted to it in perverse ways. America has always been a country where wealth is respected, and the rags-to-riches story is a fundamental part of the American idea. But the United States has never been a place where the middle class was treated with contempt. Over the past several decades, since the FIRE Economy began to reward financial over productive invention and to concentrate wealth into fewer hands, the middle class has come to be treated like second-class citizens—by the law, in the movies, on television shows. The TECI Economy celebrates all labor as honorable and worthy of respect. Everyone has a role in the TECI Economy, and everyone's contribution is vital.

TECI runs on entrepreneurs of all stripes. To make more of them, the United States has to enhance what social scientists call "human capital"—the brains that run the country. To do so, the United States needs to embark on a crash program to bring its K through 12 education up to and beyond international standards, reduce the cost of higher education, expand options to graduating high school students beyond a traditional four-year college degree, and change immigration policy to retain foreign students who come to the United States to study.

The TECI Economy needs machinists as much as it needs doctors and more than it needs lawyers. The apprenticeship education model will quickly and inexpensively retrain millions of Americans for the kinds of jobs that a productive economy requires. Why keep millions of kids on a college track if there are no jobs for them when they graduate with the twin challenges of being both trained for an outmoded economy and indebted? Help them find the entrepreneurs who will employ them while training them with hands-on experience. That on-the-job knowledge will be far more valuable than any degree they could obtain. Yes, there is an element of risk, but without risk there's little upside.

That's not to say that university education doesn't have a place in the TECI Economy. Clearly, it does. High-technology infrastructure requires advanced learning as much as it requires people to roll up their sleeves and get to work. Why do so many of the world's business and government leaders attend university in the United States? Because the United States has many of the best technology universities in the world. Hundreds of thousands of the best and the brightest come from around the world to learn at American universities, where they become the best-trained engineers, physicists, and technologists on Earth. The most entrepreneurial of them want to stay, but we send them home. This is one of the few parts of building the TECI Economy that is easy: All we have to do is modify our immigration laws to begin working for us instead of against us.

This is the bright future that I believe is possible. When I first set out on this project, I was more optimistic. TECI seems further away than it did even twelve months ago. The future was bright back when we were looking at the crisis as a forcing function for "change," before President Obama hired Larry Summers, Timothy Geithner, and other FIRE Economy insiders to rescue the old system instead of phasing it out, and before I realized how quickly peak cheap oil would be upon us. That said, TECI is out there, and we will get there.

While we work toward it, though, we'll need a firm understanding of the midterm horizon macroeconomic forecast. In chapter 5, I'll go into the phenomenon of peak cheap oil in-depth. The FIRE Economy ran on cheap oil. Now that it's getting more expensive to extract, the price of oil will have a significant impact on how we experience the next decade. Chapter 6 turns us toward larger issues of how to do the macroeconomic forecasting necessary to make wise investment decisions in a postbubble world.

PART III
—
THE MIDTERM
MACRO FORECAST

CHAPTER 5

—

PEAK CHEAP OIL

My grandfather rode a camel, my father rode a camel, I drive a
Mercedes, my son drives a Land Rover, his son will drive a Land
Rover, but his son will ride a camel.

**—RASHID BIN SAEED AL MAKTOUM, SECOND PRIME
MINISTER OF THE UNITED ARAB EMIRATES**

The FIRE Economy ran on cheap oil and cheap credit. We got cheap
oil because of the dollar cartel and because oil was easy to get. We
got cheap credit because of falling interest rates after 1980 and the
deregulation of finance after 1995. Cheap peak oil means there's no
more easy-to-get oil. It also means that pricing oil in dollars works
against America's allies' interests rather than for them, so the dollar
cartel will come apart. With interest rates at 0 percent, they have only
one way to go: up. All of the underpinnings of the FIRE Economy are
disappearing under the force of peak cheap oil. If you were born in
the United States after 1971, your entire life has been shaped by the
FIRE Economy. Everyone outside the United States has also been pro-
foundly affected. That era is over. In the transition, the government
is holding up the U.S. economy. Peak cheap oil will drive the TECI

—

Economy by forcing the country to focus on lowering energy intensity through supporting industries that develop new energy-efficient technologies, from transportation to lighting.

Gasoline and diesel, distillates of crude oil, are unique as a liquid fuel. The amount of work a gallon of these fuels can do when burned simply defies imagination. Try pushing your car ten feet on a flat driveway and you will begin to appreciate how much work the gasoline in your tank is doing when you drive. A mere ten gallons of gasoline propels a two-ton vehicle hundreds of miles up and down hills at speeds in excess of sixty miles per hour. The amount of work a liquid fuel can do by volume is referred to as its "energy density." Liquid hydrogen, by comparison, has less than one third of the energy density of gasoline. That means that you need three times as much by volume to travel the same distance, assuming both the gasoline- and hydrogen-powered engines deliver the same number of miles per pound of fuel.

What's more, gasoline is incredibly stable. You can pour it into your tank on a hot summer's day or in winter when the temperature is well below zero. Crude oil can be shipped through pipes over long distances in a wide range of temperatures and climates. This is the one and only substance like this. No other liquid that humans can dig out of the ground, refine, and pour into a tank in any climate on Earth even comes close. Every other liquid fuel has to be manufactured out of something else, then compressed, and if stored as a liquid kept at temperatures hundreds of degree below zero. You cannot transport any other fuel through hundreds of miles of pipelines. You cannot store any other fuel cheaply in unpressurized tanks.

Unfortunately, we are using up this unique and irreplaceable liquid fuel source several million times faster than it was created by nature hundreds of millions of years ago. In a little more than two human life spans, we will have used up half of all of the oil that ever existed. To compare the ancient rate of oil creation to the modern rate of oil consumption, imagine an abandoned cast-iron bathtub. Oil fills the tub one drop at a time and drips so slowly that it takes sixteen years, or five million seconds, to fill the tub.

Each second represents one year of original crude oil creation that happened through biological processes that took place over a period of approximately five hundred million years. Our simple analogy of an iron bathtub full of oil represents the whole of it, all of nature's biofuel, collected in one place. In reality, crude oil hides all over the planet. But for the convenience of our analogy, our oil-filled bathtub sits out in the open and above the ground, as easy to drain as water from a tub when you pull the plug.

But to model the rate of consumption that started in 1900, instead of opening the drain, drop a cannonball through the bottom of the tub, making a gaping hole. The dripping oil that filled the tub in five million seconds will be gone in about one second. If you are forty years old, that one second of geologic time is your lifetime so far, plus your parents' lifetimes, plus your grandparents' lifetimes.

Today oil is so hard to find and produce that energy engineers have to invent radical new technologies to find and extract it from six miles below the surface of the earth, where pressure heats the oil to five hundred degrees Fahrenheit and ordinary pipes melt trying to bring it to the surface. New technologies also allow engineers to extract petroleum from oil-rich rock deposits called shale.

The peak oil question is whether we are 0.95 or 1.1 seconds into draining our tub. That is, are we two, five, or ten years away from the beginning of a global oil production decline? And what are the implications of that inevitable decline?

An oil field is not uniform like our tub of oil. It is irregularly shaped. Think of the pattern of consumption as like drinking a soda on ice through a straw. Say there are twenty sips of milk shake in the glass. The first ten sips are easy. But after the milk shake falls to the level of the top of the ice, the last ten sips become increasingly difficult with each sip. You are forced to pull the straw up and stick it in again between the ice cubes to get at the remaining milk shake. The rate of milk shake extraction falls. Instead of a steady series of sips, each sip takes more time and effort. When you take the last few sips the liquid is next to impossible to get out of the bottom of the glass, but at least you can hold the glass up and see where the remaining milk shake is, and moving the straw around costs you nothing.

The cheap oil is the oil at the top of the reservoir. After that, oil extraction grows more difficult and expensive. When engineers extract the last oil from a reservoir, they rely on expensive exploration tools, such as satellite imaging and seismic analysis to "see" the oil. Drilling is highly capital intensive. A single deepwater dry well in Indonesia in 2004 cost $30 million.

We're at the point where we're holding up the glass of the world oil supply, searching for more to extract. Fully 83 percent of the world's major oil-producing countries—fifty-four out of sixty-five—are past peak production and in decline. Mexico and Russia are on the watch list. At iTulip we call the phenomenon of the end of cheap oil and its impact on the economy "peak cheap oil."

Oil is a finite, nonrenewable resource that we're rapidly using up. World production appears to have hit a plateau in 2004; for example, European oil production peaked in 1996, reaching a plateau that continued until 2003. After that production began to decline.

To compensate for production declines in existing oil fields, new ones have to be discovered and brought on line. Cambridge Energy Research Associates (CERA) estimates that 3.8 million barrels per day of new oil production must come on line just to maintain the current level of the global oil production plateau.

The rule of thumb is that ten billion barrels of reserves translates into approximately one million barrels per day of oil production. To produce 3.8 million barrels per day of new oil, the discovery and development of 38 billion barrels of new oil reserves are required. That means that over a ten-year period of 5 percent decline, as much oil has to be found and extracted as once existed in all of Saudi Arabia—eight times over. Engineers need to find and mine oil from the earth's crust, and squeeze it out of rocks, at a rate that is equal to the discovery of one Saudi Arabia–sized oil deposit every fifteen months. Robert Hirsh, an expert oil analyst, believes that such an engineering feat is impossible.

Hirsh's assessment is justified by the historical data on oil field discovery. More than 40 percent of oil production comes from giant oil fields. The rate of discovery of giant fields peaked in the 1960s. While giant fields are still being discovered, the rate of discovery has fallen from over 120 per decade in the 1960s, to 24 per decade of the 1980s, to 9 between 2000 and 2007.

During this fifty-year period of declining discovery, the technology for oil exploration was vastly improved, with satellite and other tools revealing deposits hidden below the land and oceans. As shallow, conventional oil fields deplete at a rate of 5 percent per year, optimistically, new oil must come from a combination of a small number of giant as yet undiscovered unconventional oil fields and from a large number of smaller oil deposits.

Hirsh explains another fact about hydrocarbons that few of us appreciate: We rely on them not only for transportation, but for many other industrial processes and materials as well. If you look around the room you are in, you will be hard-pressed to find many objects that were not either made out of or manufactured using hydrocarbons. The big question then is how many of these products—from plastics to lubricants to jet fuel—can be made with substitutes, and at what cost.

If hydrocarbons are about to become rare, the most obvious solution to keep them from becoming extinct is to use less for transportation, so that we have more left for making products, such as plastics, that can be manufactured only using hydrocarbons. But how? The existing fleet of liquid fuel–consuming vehicles, and generators that depend on liquid fuels, number in the hundreds of millions. If the end of the production plateau is upon us, how can these possibly be converted to run on nonliquid fuels within ten years or less?

Hirsh argues that the only practical solutions are conservation and rationing, wider use of heavy oils, more intensive oil recovery from existing fields, and the conversion of natural gas and coal to liquids. Yet, following Hirsh's own calculations, even if all of these methods of oil depletion mitigation are applied, assuming the optimistic 5 percent median annual global oil production decline rate, the world will still experience an oil shortage of 30 percent compared to current consumption rates. Mitigation that reduces demand—the size of the hole in the bottom of the tub of oil—only compensates for a fraction of the decline in production.

The upshot is this: Just like the milk shake in the glass of ice, our last five sips of oil will be more and more difficult to find and produce over time. Oil engineers will not be able to locate and extract the oil as fast as before. Yet demand for oil will remain high, because our transportation systems depend on it. The price will rise, and the hole in the bottom of our tub will get smaller.

In economic terms, higher oil prices means that the global economy will shrink. Hirsh's 2008 analysis of the impact of rising oil prices on economic growth revealed an approximate 1 percent decline in GDP per 1 percent decline in the oil supply. The 30 percent decline in oil supply in the ten years following the end of the plateau in oil production at 5 percent per year implies a 30 percent drop in GDP in a decade. During the first three years of the Great Depression, between 1930 and 1934, U.S. GDP declined 24 percent. Peak oil implies a per-capita economic decline even more severe than the Great Depression, although the economic decline may be more gradual.

Hirsh states that the trajectory of the economic decline caused by declining oil production is unknowable because of the interaction of the economy and investment in oil exploration and production. Our analysis from early 2009 suggests that the collision of the FIRE Economy and peak cheap oil will produce a series of economic booms and busts; the 30 percent decline will occur in an oscillation of rising prices, recession, falling demand, rising demand, rising prices, and recession.

THE PEAK CHEAP OIL MODEL

The timing of the economic oscillations of peak cheap oil is unpredictable, as is the extent of oil price increases and declines in recessions. Short-term factors include excess inventories due to global recession, as we have today; future supply shocks, due to underinvestment that we expect to see between 2012 and 2015; anti–asset price deflation

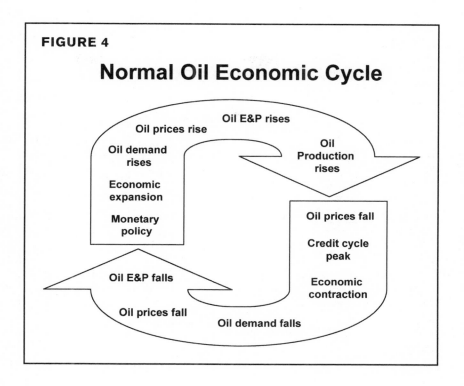

FIGURE 4

Normal Oil Economic Cycle

monetary policy; anti–oil cost-push inflation monetary policy; and dollar reserve status changes.

The first peak cheap oil cycle has replaced the asset bubble cycle. To understand the peak cheap oil cycle framework, it's worth reviewing the normal workings of oil prices, supply and demand, in a credit cycle before we reached peak cheap oil production limits in 2004.

Before peak cheap oil, the price of oil and the oil industry's response to it was driven by economic expansions and contractions that were themselves a function of the credit cycle.

Starting from the economic policy response to recession at the bottom of the "Monetary policy" stage of the Normal Economic Oil Cycle shown in the diagram above, the economy begins to expand. As the economy expands, oil demand rises, and oil prices rise. Higher prices induce energy companies to increase oil exploration and production

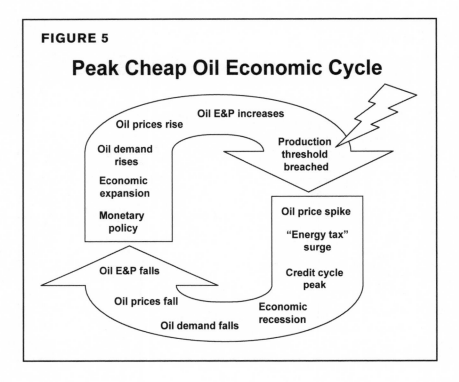

FIGURE 5

Peak Cheap Oil Economic Cycle

Oil E&P increases

Oil prices rise

Oil demand rises

Economic expansion

Monetary policy

Production threshold breached

Oil price spike

"Energy tax" surge

Credit cycle peak

Oil E&P falls

Oil prices fall

Economic recession

Oil demand falls

(E&P). Then the oil supply rises, and prices fall. Eventually the economy reaches a peak of credit growth in the credit cycle and turns down. The economy turns down or even goes into recession. Oil demand declines, prices fall, and oil E&P declines. Monetary policy then restarts the next period of economic growth. This is the cycle that the U.S. economy has experienced for decades, although it was exaggerated by the asset bubble cycle of the FIRE Economy beginning in the early 1980s.

Starting in 2004, this all changed.

The fundamental change—around the time that the housing bubble–financed economic "recovery" was picking up steam—is that world oil production peaked and reached a plateau even as the economy expanded and oil demand continued to rise. This produced a sharp increase in oil prices in 2007 and 2008, later amplified by investment banks and hedge funds—who do nothing better than take a trend and push it to the nth degree. Just as in the 1970s, the oil price spike diverted household and business expenditure from goods and services in the economy; an oil price spike acts like an added "energy tax" on the economy. The 2008 oil price spike accelerated the recession that began in late 2007, a year after the start of the collapse of the housing bubble.

Starting with this first peak cheap oil price spike, from there on out every economic expansion will be throttled by a spike in oil prices, as the production threshold of around eighty-five million barrels per day is reached, and—over time—shrinks. Each cycle will produce a higher oil spike, and each application of orthodox counter–credit cycle monetary policy will put a higher floor on oil prices.

What kind of price spikes can we expect? The impact of peak oil in the United States in 1970 is indicative.

Oil prices began to increase coincident with the peak in U.S. pro-

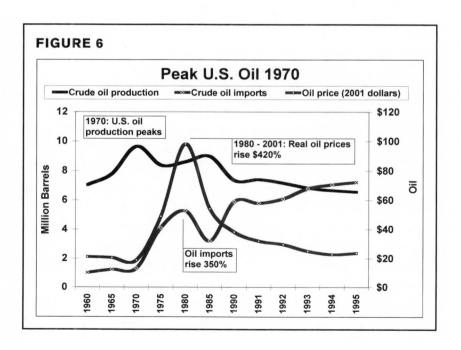

FIGURE 6

Peak U.S. Oil 1970

━━Crude oil production ━✕━Crude oil imports ━━Oil price (2001 dollars)

1970: U.S. oil production peaks

1980 - 2001: Real oil prices rise $420%

Oil imports rise 350%

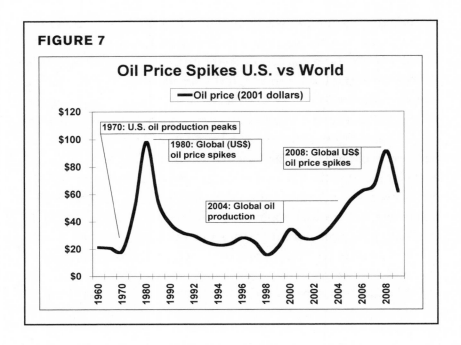

FIGURE 7

Oil Price Spikes U.S. vs World

—Oil price (2001 dollars)

1970: U.S. oil production peaks

1980: Global (US$) oil price spikes

2008: Global US$ oil price spikes

2004: Global oil production

duction in 1970, as oil imports started a steady 450 percent increase over the decade that followed. As production fell and imports increased, oil priced in dollars increased more or less in proportion. Adjusted for inflation, average annual oil prices increased 520 percent in inflation-adjusted terms between 1970 and 1980. The oil price spike produced a recession and a wave of double-digit inflation that the Federal Reserve addressed with double-digit rate hikes starting in 1980.

The recession decimated oil demand and prices plummeted. In parallel, the United States and its allies developed the dollar cartel, that system of U.S. Treasury debt trades that created artificial global demand for dollars; the price of oil, the reciprocal of dollars, declined continuously. The dollar and oil became intricately tied, with dollar demand and price driving the oil price.

On a global scale, prices increased 234 percent from the 2002 recession low of $27 average annual to $91 average annual in 2008.

You can expect a series of similar increases to occur in each peak cheap oil cycle. The next cycle may take the price to approximately $160, between 2011 and 2012, and then it will decline to approximately $80 in the recession that follows, based on calculations we did in late 2008.

Economies of developing countries are more seriously affected by high oil prices than those of developed countries. A brief oil spike to $150 in 2008 led to food riots from Egypt to Haiti. This now forgotten story reveals the outsized impact of expensive oil on the poor. The real world impact of high oil prices on food prices has political implications, even within the United States. If 11 percent of Americans are on food stamps in the first peak cheap oil cycle, how many will need government support after the next cycle?

Even the economies of developed countries can be severely impacted by high oil prices; the bottom 50 percent of the population is especially vulnerable. Gasoline at five dollars a gallon would put an

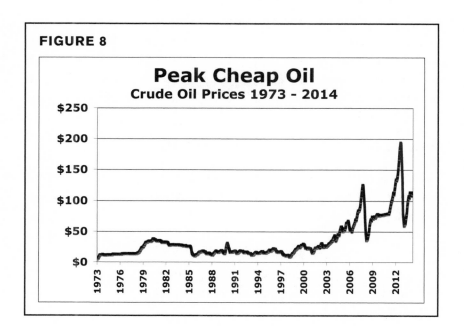

FIGURE 8

Peak Cheap Oil
Crude Oil Prices 1973 - 2014

even greater strain on America's underdeveloped public transportation system than in 2008, when gasoline briefly reached four dollars.

A peak cheap oil cycle is inherently inflationary. Higher energy prices raise input costs for all kinds of businesses, such as food production and public transportation. These costs have to be passed on to consumers, to buyers of food and users of public transportation, or these activities become uneconomical for producers. They can't lose money on every apple or train seat and make it up in volume.

If consumers do not have the income to pay the higher costs, then demand falls—which is another way of saying that Americans won't be able to buy food or travel as they could before. The higher prices of oil and gasoline will set the prices of everything else. Anyone who is already living a marginal existence, paycheck to paycheck, gets pushed over the edge financially. Millions will move from upper middle class to lower, and millions more from lower to poverty, with each peak cheap oil cycle.

If you think it all through, peak cheap oil means not only high inflation, but also exploding government debt, as an ever wider range of essential economic activity becomes uneconomical and governments will be forced to subsidize them or face the ire of voters. Five million Americans are collecting unemployment insurance. Who pays the insurance? Businesses do.

PEAK CHEAP OIL COMPLICATIONS

Complicating our relatively simple peak cheap oil cycle model are four major trends of varying duration that increase the uncertainty of the forecast.

1. dollar decommissioning
2. national depletion-management policies
3. rapid depletion of U.S. natural gas supply
4. deep-sea oil

DOLLAR DECOMMISSIONING

The 2008 U.S. financial crisis energized a global political movement that had started decades ago to end the U.S.-centric dollar-based global monetary system.

The decommissioning of the dollar as a global reserve currency has negative implications not only for the affordability of oil imported into the United States. It means that the United States and its allies will, sooner rather than later, begin to pay true market prices for oil, not prices discounted by a currency that is overvalued due to artificial demand. The U.S. dollar, structurally overvalued since the early 1980s, has for decades led oil producers to extract and sell oil at below market prices. As the dollar cartel winds down, so too will the exorbitant privilege of buying a nonrenewable resource with the currency of a nation that does not have to earn a foreign exchange.

After the great crash of 2008, the world's governments accelerated the process of ending the dollar cartel. Moves to gradually replace the dollar's role as the primary reserve currency are gaining momentum, most recently with the decision by the government of Turkey to conduct its oil trade in euros instead of dollars.

I do not believe the dollar will crash dramatically unless the United States experiences a sudden stop, an event that leads to a sudden reversal of capital inflows, a sovereign debt and currency crisis. That may happen, but more likely the dollar dies the death of a thousand cuts, with one country after another reducing the dollar's role in international trade, especially oil, resulting in a gradual decline in the dollar by another 40 percent to 50 percent from 2008 levels.

NATIONAL DEPLETION-MANAGEMENT POLICIES

As the reality of peak oil arrives, the governments of oil-producing countries will seek to increase their control of their remaining oil resources. Today, around 85 percent of oil and gas reserves are held by state-owned companies, up from 50 percent twenty years ago.

Oil production declined in Russia soon after nationalization. The apparent correlation between nationalization and falling production in several instances conforms to the belief that private markets are more efficient at exploration and production, known in the industry as E&P, than are government-owned oil companies, yet causation is hard to establish. In the case of Russia, where nationalization led many Western oil E&P experts to leave the country, the case can be more readily made. But in countries such as Mexico, where the state oil company, Pemex, has been in operation for decades, oil production declines confirm the reality that governments can deplete a finite national resource to reach a peak and decline in national oil production just as well as the private sector did in the United States in the 1970s. The second trend, toward even greater nationalization of energy resources, will lead to a rationing of oil exports as part of a growing trend toward depletion management.

This is not good news for oil importers such as the United States. It's worth noting that a poll of fifteen hundred Canadian citizens in the summer of 2005 revealed that nearly half favor nationalization of Canadian energy resources. Since the United States relies on Canada more than any other country for oil imports, if the Canadian government enacted an energy nationalization policy, the United States will need the enormous supply of natural gas from shale "discoveries" trumpeted in the pages of the *Wall Street Journal* and the *New York Times*. Too bad they're a pipe dream.

Governments are becoming more aware of the value of nonrenewable national energy resources. As they do, oil-producing countries will sell less of them to oil-consuming countries such as the United States. The way they will do that is through the markets, by allowing the global market price of oil to rise for exported oil while subsidizing domestic oil consumption. In fact, that's what most oil-producing countries do today.

The significance of the trend to us as investors is that it is but one of several factors that will lead to higher oil prices in the future, even if enough new unconventional oil is discovered to counter the 5 percent annual loss in conventional sources. There may be enough oil, but nonproducers will get less of it. We do not see the trend reversing, but instead intensifying, from here on out.

RAPID DEPLETION OF U.S. NATURAL GAS SUPPLY

The FIRE sector and its media trumpet natural gas as the great hope for U.S. oil independence. They argue that new technologies will allow rapid extraction of U.S. reserves via new gas extraction technologies. But geology and physics cannot be trumped by finance. The implications are short-term bearish and long-term bullish for gas, if by "bullish" we mean high prices. Banks and operators can make a killing on debt and equity. The Wall Street trade press is in full operation, selling this deal like it did the "new economy" in 1999, during the tech bubble, and the "dream of home ownership" in 2005, during the housing bubble.

Will new technologies allow us to replace oil with natural gas? As a technology industry executive, I admit I am susceptible to the technology case. (If you doubt that claim, go back and reread the TECI chapter.) After all, it has been correct and defied the technopessimists for most of my adult life. Yet time after time the data lead one to conclude that no matter how brilliantly we look for something that isn't there, we won't find it, and if we figure out how to increase the rate of extraction of that which is there, we only move out the day of reckoning.

Peter A. Dea, president and CEO of Cirque Resources LP, asserts that the United States has one hundred years of natural gas reserves buried in the rocks, and that new natural gas extraction technology will allow us to dispense with foreign oil, save the environment from dirty coal, and put a chicken in every pot by providing millions of new jobs.

The game changer? Gas from shale. Not only can this new technology get more gas out of rocks we know about, it can help us find rocks we didn't know were there. A large number of small, uneconomical

shales are yet to be discovered. Why? Because small means uneconomical. Eventually higher prices will fix that problem, making uneconomical shale economical, Dea argues. Claims of more nonrenewable
fossil fuel reserves are not exaggerated, but the economic conditions
that are necessary to make them worthwhile mean that oil and gas
prices must go much higher, and that spells trouble for the economy.

American and Canadian geologists I spoke with rolled their eyes
when I asked them later if Dea's "many undiscovered shales" assertion
held water. Proved reserves are about one tenth of "supply"—or so the
story goes. What about the other 90 percent? No estimates of margin
of error are applied to justify how a ten-year supply of proven reserves
becomes a one-hundred-year total supply that weans the United States
off off-continent oil.

Art Berman, director of Labyrinth Consulting Services, presents
the counterargument. His slides may lack the slick formatting that
made Peter's easy to watch—the academic and technically trained
peak oil crew have a thing or two to learn about sales and marketing,
since being right is not enough—but they were packed with much ug-
lier data.

The upshot of Berman's case is that, if it sounds too good to be
true, it probably is. Can any strategy combine low risk and high reward? Can the sum of high capital costs plus low gas prices equal high
profits? Only 38 percent of the projected total production of 26 trillion
cubic feet, or tcf, can ever be realized at any cost, and only 30 percent
of that—13 percent of the estimated resource base—is commercially
viable. So far $35 billion has been spent on drilling and leasing alone
to get ten tcf. To get at the other sixteen will cost an additional $80
billion.

In the gas minibubble, engineering companies that inflate the case
for it are playing the role that the ratings agencies and home appraisers
played during the housing mortgage bubble—selling inflated ratings
and valuations. If an engineering firm declines to offer inflated-reserve
and low-decline-rate estimates, another firm will take the job. If ex-

ecutives of operating companies don't play along, they will be replaced by ones who will better "look after the shareholders' interests." I saw this happen over and over again in the technology industry during the tech bubble.

Berman has identified a self-reinforcing asset inflation cycle, the hallmark of an asset bubble: a rush to lease, followed by drilling, followed by further inflated reserves estimates, followed by higher valuations that lead to more debt and equity issuance, leading to a rush to lease.

He does not blame either the operators or the banks for playing this game, just as I didn't blame the VCs or executives that ran the tech firms, or even the banks and other players that got sucked into the housing bubble. As long as the revolving door exists between the regulators and the industries they are charged to regulate—as long as the U.S. government remains captured by the FIRE industry—these bubbles will recur.

There's an additional problem with the gas minibubble: Rather than leaving behind a useful communications infrastructure, as the telecom bubble did, it has the potential to be even more macroeconomically damaging than the housing bubble that left behind millions of houses to rot on their foundations from South Florida to Arizona.

If the United States cannot run on LNG as a replacement for liquid fuels—and it can't—we're back to looking at the oil supply.

DEEP-SEA OIL

The idea that tens of billions of barrels of oil lie deep under the sea awaiting discovery by new technology is appealing but not supported by the evidence. Oil discovery techniques have not improved markedly over the past ten years. The reason is that techniques invented decades ago have been perfected since then. We won't run on deep-sea oil any more than we'll run on natural gas.

The technical challenge of "seeing" undersea oil is that the thick salt layer covering these deposits severely attenuates and distorts the seismic signals used to measure and map the fields. Accurately imaging and placing structures in three-dimensional space deep in the earth so they can be targeted with an oil drill bit requires huge computing power.

As one energy expert told me, the presalt reservoirs that exist deep in the earth's crust were unlocked by Moore's Law. In 1965, Gordon E. Moore predicted an annual doubling of computer power and an attendant decrease in computing costs. An enormous increase in desktop workstation computing power in the early 1990s cut the cost of running sophisticated seismic processing algorithms by orders of magnitude.

What used to take enormous amounts of money and several days running a Cray supercomputer in a glass house owned by one of the world's largest oil companies can, since the mid-1990s, be done in hours on a workstation, or even on a personal computer. The number of geophysicists and geologists that have access to this capability has multiplied exponentially; an army versus a handful of creative minds have been working the problem. The ensuing raft of presalt discoveries in places like Angola and the Gulf of Suez over the past fifteen years is the result.

The fact is that the army of oil explorers and their powerful computers have already found most of the oil, first in shallow fields starting in the mid-1850s, then deep in the earth since the early 1980s, now deeper than 1980s' oil geologists could ever have imagined. Oil cannot exist at even greater depths for reasons of physics: The heat and pressure turn the oil into gas, and gas, as we shall see later in this report, depletes differently than oil, and has much less desirable economics.

The Earth and its oil are like a beach combed by treasure seekers with metal detectors looking for ancient lost coins. The metal-detector technology can keep getting better, and the detectors can get cheaper, until the beach is covered with treasure hunters, but eventually all of the coins are found, because only so many ancient coins were ever dropped in the first place.

Even if the oil exists, it really is technically very challenging to get at. The cost of deepwater drilling is much higher than shallow-water or onshore exploration, and the risks are high. A deepwater oil rig costs up to $200,000 to rent for a day, five times that of a shallow-water rig. The first deepwater well in Malaysia, drilled in 2009 by France's Total, Petronas and Austria's OMV, turned out to be a dry hole. The cost: $30 million plus months of hard labor.

As daunting as deepwater oil E&P are, history has been unkind to oil E&P technology naysayers. Where there is a will, there's a way. Initially, deepwater oil drilling technology was expensive. Cost is largely a function of the limited number of deepwater oil rigs. That's about to change.

The assertion that another nine hundred billion barrels of oil exists below the salt is just not credible. There is no question that large oil deposits exist in the deep water off Brazil and many countries around the world. But how much oil is there, really? HRT Petroleum president Marcio Rocha Mello claims that 130 billion barrels of deepwater oil exist off Brazil, but the U.S. Department of Energy estimates that only 180 billion barrels of deepwater oil exist in total.

One energy expert I spoke with noted that ultradeepwater fields in Brazil and the Gulf of Mexico surprised engineers who did not believe that hydrocarbons at those depths, pressures, and temperatures could still be oil rather than petroleum turned entirely into natural gas. Some of the fields in these areas do contain very large hydrocarbon reservoirs, but there is a big economic difference between finding valuable oil and finding less valuable gas at those depths. The last two deepwater drills in 2009 by the Brazilian oil company BG in the Santos Basin off Brazil found gas, not oil.

Mello claims that the hydrocarbons haven't been cracked because the salt layer has acted as a heat sink for the underlying organic source rock. Perhaps that is true, but that remains a theory that has not been proven, and it may only apply to the very specific case of the region off the coast of Brazil, not a new principle of oil geology that can be used to estimate the potential size of deepwater oil deposits globally.

At what oil price is deepwater oil E&P technology economical? A report released in December 2008 by oil research and consulting firm Wood Mackenzie forecast a dramatic slowdown in Gulf of Mexico activities in 2009 if oil prices remained below fifty dollars per barrel without an accompanying drop in development costs. That forecast applies only to the larger oil discoveries. The report goes on to note that smaller discoveries that looked economical at one hundred dollars per barrel or higher oil prices might be shelved. Indeed, that is exactly what has happened.

Andrew McBarnet, writing for *Offshore Engineer* magazine in October 2009, concludes:

> In a sense, little of the current macroeconomic debate should be relevant to E&P decision making. Long-term investments in oil and gas projects from the exploration phase to production can take up to 10 years to realize, especially now that easy oil is no longer available. No one seriously argues that in 10 years' time demand for hydrocarbon products will have somehow collapsed and that oil prices will be in terminal decline. Precisely the opposite. You don't have to be a Peak Oil advocate to venture the opinion that oil prices in another decade will have skyrocketed, as a result of scarcity and surging demand. The question is whether the price that oil producers can charge for the product will be high enough to allow them to recoup the capital costs of production. One of the greatest paradoxes of peak cheap oil may be that diminishing oil supplies reduce rather than increase oil company profits, because the capital costs of producers rise faster than the incomes of consumers. If consumers cannot afford higher prices, oil companies cannot pass them on. Once oil companies understand this I expect they will be major proponents of the TECI Economy that seeks to reduce oil demand by reducing energy intensity.

CONCLUSIONS

Even using the most optimistic assessment of decline rates of cheap oil fields, substitutes for crude oil cannot be manufactured at a rate that exceeds the rate of decline of cheap oil and will contribute little to reducing the inflationary pressures during the price spike phases of the peak cheap oil cycle.

Peak cheap oil itself will lead to a series of economic recessions that will drive major increases in government spending to ease the impact on food and transportation costs. The U.S. public debt to GDP ratio may exceed 20 percent in the next cycle, up from 12.3 percent in fiscal year 2009. Given $60 trillion in total contingent liabilities of public debt and entitlement programs, the United States may in this period exceed a fiscal deficit threshold that allows the United States to maintain its current account imbalance, leading to a current account crisis, a sovereign bond crisis, and a dollar crisis.

BEST-CASE SCENARIO:
MANAGED PEAK CHEAP OIL PROCESS

- The FIRE Economy gradually fades away, real estate prices fall, and debt is written down to manageable levels.
- Governments of net oil producing and net oil consuming nations cooperate worldwide to manage allocation of remaining cheap oil.
- National governments move quickly to accelerate market processes and shorten the natural market development period to drive the rapid adoption of more fuel-efficient plug-in hybrid diesel and LNG vehicles by ending the chicken-and-egg conundrum with subsidies to develop fueling stations and build vehicles.
- The dollar declines gradually from an index value of 75 to 40 between 2009 and 2015 as it is decommissioned by U.S. trade partners from its role as a primary reserve currency.

- The United States accelerates its high-technology export trade capability that allows it to earn foreign exchange.
- Net government and private savings and investment rises.

WORST-CASE SCENARIO:
CHAOTIC PEAK CHEAP OIL PROCESS

- Pro–FIRE Economy policies are pursued; trillions in government subsidies are allocated in an attempt to maintain real estate prices to avoid writing down or writing off debt.
- This, in combination with the cost of subsidizing food and transportation, causes the United States to exceed a fiscal deficit to GDP threshold and experience a sudden stop during the next peak cheap oil cycle. The dollar declines from an index value of 75 to under 40 over a few months, decommissioning the dollar as a primary reserve currency in a single, catastrophic event.
- Governments of net oil producing and net oil consuming nations fight over the remaining cheap oil, with major wars involving large areas of the world.
- The long market development time for fuel-efficient plug-in hybrid diesel and LNG vehicles to replace the current fleet is lengthened by economic distress, exaggerating the demand impact of economic recoveries and the resulting price spike during the recovery phase of the next peak cheap oil cycle.
- The U.S. fails to develop its high-technology export trade capability and must resort to sales of valuable assets, such as its technology industry, to finance imports.

CHAPTER 6

—

ECONOMIC AND MARKET FORECASTING IN A POSTBUBBLE WORLD

All of the great leaders have had one characteristic in common: it was the willingness to confront unequivocally the major anxiety of their people in their time. This, and not much else, is the essence of leadership.

—JOHN KENNETH GALBRAITH,
THE AGE OF UNCERTAINTY

The opportunity for a new administration in Washington to use the 2008 financial and economic crisis as a political forcing function for painful structural change has been lost. The Obama administration could have said, "We've been living on borrowed money for too long. We borrowed from other countries and from future generations and lived large off of fake wealth manufactured by public and private credit that made asset price bubbles in stocks and housing. The system of private credit and money that made this bogus money and fake wealth is broken. If we keep trying to compensate for it with government cash and credit, we'll run out of both, and our bond market and currency will collapse. We have to shift our economy to increase saving and investment and pay down our debt. We also have to gradually

—

devalue the dollar. Our living standards will fall. Your income will not buy the same quantity and quality of goods and services as before. In fact, you are seeing this already. But after ten years of sacrifice, we will have our house in order. I believe in the American people. I know we can do it."

That speech never happened. Rather than use our nation's remaining foreign and domestic government credit and credibility to build a solid foundation for capital formation, and to make our economy more competitive by improving energy infrastructure and bolstering productive enterprises, the new administration perpetuated the FIRE-friendly policies of previous administrations in a desperate bid to restart the old economy. We had a change in leadership, but FIRE sector interests still dominate the legislative process and public policy. The bailouts of AIG and GM, the "cash for clunkers" program, the Fed's purchases of asset-backed securities, the $250 bribe doled out to seniors, among other policies, make the administration's political orientation clear.

Despite the right-wing hue and cry, the Obama administration's agenda doesn't lie anywhere close to socialism. Socialism is public and worker ownership and administration of producers and resources. The philosophy behind it is that equal access to production and resources and egalitarian methods of compensation result in a more healthy and fair society.

Socialism doesn't work for two reasons. First, government cannot allocate resources efficiently. No government administrators have the superhuman ability to make all of the micro decisions that make up an efficient allocation of resources by markets. Second, running a successful, competitive business that grows and employs workers is many times harder than working for one, and it takes a special talent that not everyone possesses. If the job were not better compensated than other jobs, who'd do it?

No one will do it for the same compensation that everyone else gets. A capitalist state that becomes socialist can run for a few years off the money, talent, and will of the men and women who used to run productive businesses in previous years. But, as Maggie Thatcher once famously said, eventually you run out of other people's money. I'd add that you also run out of passion and talent. It leaves. In a few years the economy achieves an equal distribution of poverty and settles into a malaise. But in that malaise, the seeds of a new movement for entrepreneurship are planted, and the cycle begins anew. This has been going on for many centuries. The only way to grow the pie is through open competition among entrepreneurs with equal access to the primary factors of production for a modern economy: educated and experienced talent and capital.

Most of the nation's money and credit have been concentrated on reviving the FIRE sectors, those sectors of the economy that contribute little to American competitiveness but instead siphon off cash flows from businesses and households via economic rents—interest payments, fees, and insurance premiums. Meanwhile, the productive industries that create those cash flows—the businesses that earn profits and the households that earn income—are still dropping like flies, as the latest unemployment, business bankruptcy, and tax collection data shows.

That's not socialism. What we have here, as former lead economist for the International Monetary Fund Simon Johnson says, is a financial oligarchy. It has resulted from decades of concentration of political power in the hands of finance, insurance, and real estate interests who have used financial power through political action committees, lobbyists, campaign contributions, and other means to influence legislation that benefits their interests, which in turn further increases their financial power and political influence.

With all of this as background, you can begin to understand why markets are behaving as they are and where this is all going. Pro–FIRE Economy policies have reduced our capacity for capital formation since the early 1980s, but by no means destroyed it. We have an enormous stock of competitive industries in the United States to build on as a platform for a new, vibrant economy—the TECI Economy. But we have also developed a large external debt position that limits our ability as a nation to make decisions in our long-term national self-interest. In addition to putting FIRE Economy interests ahead of the interests of productive industries that make American more competitive, our government is becoming more like Argentina's. Our leaders are turning into custodians of the foreign debt.

The risk that foreign lenders may suddenly sell Treasury bonds and crash the dollar is exceeded only by the risk that they won't. When a nation takes on as much debt as the United States has from foreign governments, political influence naturally follows. Because of our large external debt position, foreign governments are motivated to influence our elections and legislation just as domestic FIRE industries interests influence our government to look after their interests. They want to make sure that they are repaid, and they don't want to be repaid with devalued dollars.

I started watching bubbles in 1998. My perspective is of someone who spent time at the heart of one of the bubbles—tech—first as an investor, and then as the CEO of one of the companies we invested in, riding out the aftermath of the crash. I was able to invest in bubbles to generate returns on my own account (and share what I learned with my readers at iTulip.com). I have a deep disdain for efficient market theory. You can't leave money in one asset class for many decades, as modern portfolio theory argues, and hope to earn good risk-adjusted returns. Asset allocations cannot be maintained through decades that span periods of major macroeconomic change, including asset bubbles and a global economic power shift from West to East. The name of the game is moving assets from one asset class to another, not quickly, but slowly, as macroeconomic conditions change—once every ten years, say.

The uniquely American bubble system that drove the tech and housing bubbles in the United States depended on government, mostly in the form of asset price inflation monetary policy, nonenforcement of securities and banking regulations, and the sales and marketing of the product by the media, as I explained in the 2008 *Harper's* article "The Next Bubble."

I don't read anyone else's market and economic forecasts until they are at least half a year old. That may strike some readers as odd, but there's a method to the madness. If I stick to my own primary research and analysis, then I can be certain that if my analysis agrees with the analysis of others, it's because I have reached the same conclusions independently. And one conclusion that all of us have come to is that the era of predictable, big, macroeconomically significant bubble booms and busts is over. I should have called my *Harper's* article "The Last Bubble."

Timing asset bubbles is trivial compared to predicting how markets will respond to an economy that is so heavily influenced by and dependent on monetary and fiscal policy. In 2009 we entered a new era where the skills of a Soviet-era Kremlinologist are needed to forecast markets. What will the Kremlin do next? How will markets react? Who knows?

Debt deflation will continue for many years in the United States, but not in the form or for as long as it lasted in the 1930s, and certainly not as long as it has in Japan since 1990. Although we started in 2008 at nearly the same point as Japan did in 1990, with public debt outstanding at 60 percent of GDP, as a net debtor and capital importer the United States will run out of foreign credit long before our public debt to GDP ratio gets even close to Japan's today, 200 percent of GDP.

If U.S. creditors force our hand and demand that the United States cut deficits and raise interest rates before the U.S. economy is self-sustaining without stimuli, commonly known as "austerity measures," we then enter a new era—of "Argentina with American characteristics." Rate hikes and spending cuts will produce the outcome that foreign creditors fear: slowing economic growth; falling capital inflows; rising interest rates; and a rapidly depreciating dollar.

The "seven lean years" that follow will be reminiscent of the 1970s. Not everything will go wrong, but it may feel that way compared to the picture-perfect era of low inflation, low unemployment, and high productivity of the 1990s. As in the inglorious 1970s, some things will go well and others badly.

There are really only four trends we need to watch to understand the future direction of the S&P. The first is final sales to domestic producers. Businesses have achieved most if not all of their earnings growth from cost cutting. The bulls will say that this positions them for rapid profits growth when demand picks up. That's true, but if businesses are not growing sales, stock prices cannot continue to rise.

The second is personal consumption expenditures. If PCE does not continue to rise, sales will not rise and stock prices will not rise. So far all we have is a "cash for clunkers" bounce and some irrational exuberance. If PCE turns down or even continues to churn sideways, stocks will go nowhere.

In the long-term forecast, the shocker among our economic charts is in our most reliable economic forecasting measure since 1998, median duration of unemployment (MDU). After a dip in August 2009, it went up again in September and has been rising ever since, even into the spring of 2010 when the economy is reportedly recovering. That means that companies are still not hiring. Not good. That's shocking this far into an economic downturn. If we look at the number of job openings, we see that they hit an all-time low in September 2009. An increase in job openings tends to lag recovery by several years. That means MDU still has a long way to go before peaking.

The fourth is government spending. All the spending noted above gets us is a modest increase in GDP growth, a dubious measure of economic output. What happens when our creditors force the Fed to raise interest rates and Congress to cut spending? By the spring of 2010, China is openly demanding that the United States reduce its fiscal deficit. The only way to do that is to raise taxes or cut spending. In March 2010, bond rating agency Moody's warned that the United States faces a downgrading of its Treasury bonds below the triple A rating that earns the bonds their famed "risk free" status.

The U.S. economy is famously driven by consumption. Personal consumption expenditure accounts for more than 70 percent of GDP. That consumption is not financed out of savings, but primarily out of income and credit. Household debt repayment for consumption competes with many other demands on household cash flows, such as mortgage and student loan repayment. If you think of debt that results from the use of household credit for consumption as variable and mortgage debt as fixed, you can understand why U.S. households are uniquely vulnerable to unemployment compared to households in countries that do not operate this way. That's why the United States is not recovering—despite the official claim that the recession ended in June 2009—while many other countries' economies are. In April 2009 I began forecasting positive economic growth in the third quarter of the same year, when the impact of the stimulus peaked. The question remains, Will that growth become self-sustaining? Without personal credit growth or jobs growth, that strikes us as implausible. One thing's for sure: If the stimulus spending does not produce self-sustained growth, continued government spending will bankrupt us. The Congressional Budget Office announced in March 2009 that the budget deficit was expected to hit a record $1.4 trillion of 13.2 percent of GDP in 2009, this only fourteen months after projecting a deficit of only 4 percent of GDP for 2009. In January 2010, the CBO projected a deficit in excess of $1.3 trillion for 2010, $100 billion less than 2009. U.S. creditors will not put up with this for long before they demand budget cuts, higher interest rates on the debt they hold when it is rolled over— totaling one third of all outstanding Treasury bonds—or both.

Most Americans can't afford to be unemployed but for a few months or face bankruptcy, so they take few risks that might result in an interruption or reduction in income, such as trying their hand at starting a company or joining a high risk venture like a start-up company. This effect is amplified during economic recessions. And it's not like every household can simply decide to avoid debt. A person without a degree beyond a high school diploma will struggle near the poverty level in the United States, so education is mandatory to get above the poverty line. Yet the median income in the United States is forty-five thousand dollars; the majority of families cannot afford to write a check to pay their children's college tuition. Median tuition is now 60 percent of annual income versus 20 percent in 1980, so student loans are the only option for students who do not qualify for a scholarship. For most Americans, the uneducated are doomed to a life of poverty, the educated to a mountain of debt. The FIRE Economy does not give most Americans attractive options outside a life of debt serfdom.

The parasite, the FIRE Economy that extracts rents from the productive economy, gets the bulk of the taxpayer stimulus support while the host, the productive economy, continues to shrink.

Everyone on the contrarian economics and finance circuit has been waiting since last summer for a new period of deflation as occurred in early 2009 to knock stocks and commodities down in a fresh wave of deleveraging and panic selling like the one we saw in late 2008 and early 2009. They want another chance to "buy the dip" in a secular uptrend in commodities. U.S. stocks and commodities may correlate short term, as they did during the deleveraging that happened during the panic. That's when investors sold anything and everything to raise cash.

Many analysts at the time said the crash marked the beginning of a 1930s-style liquidity trap that they'd long predicted. They got it wrong, although they'll never admit it. Governments don't do deflation spirals anymore, not since the abandonment of the gold standard by governments worldwide in the 1930s. And the Fed knew that the most effective way to get the U.S. economy out of a liquidity trap is to not fall into one in the first place. You may run across the term "deflation scare" to refer to the period of panic selling. It is not a useful concept. Market participants expect either rising or falling future inflation. They aren't scared of either. If by deflation scare the users of this phrase mean "a false expectation of future deflation," then the idea is tautological. It asserts that markets falsely expect deflation in a deflation scare. How will we know the deflation expectation was false? Because the deflation doesn't happen.

A more logical way to think about the dynamic is that the majority of market participants are deflationists; that is, they do not understand the nature of asset price inflation and deflation in the FIRE Economy, its relationship to commodity price deflation in the productive economy, monetary policy with respect to each, and the impact of monetary policy. Now the question is, After the past two asset price crashes, the first in 2000 and the second in 2008, have the majority of market participants caught on to the fact that monetary policy is now firmly on the side of preventing the ship from capsizing at all costs, even if it means a weaker dollar, higher commodity prices, and even more public debt? If so, we may not see any commodity price deflation at all in the market panic. We may skip the brief deflation step entirely.

The dollar may have experienced a short-term spike, but unless one believes that the United States and the global economy is about to undergo a spontaneous restructuring that causes a rebirth of the dollar reminiscent of the early 1980s, during the start of the FIRE Economy, who cares what the dollar does over a quarter or two? Not me—I'm not a day trader—so daily or even annual price changes are only interesting if they occur as part of a process that can be explained and forecast to occur over a distinct timeframe, such as the first year of the debt deflation bear market that began in 2008 and will continue much as Japan's bear market in stocks has for nearly twenty years since 1990. Until we elect politicians who will bite the bullet and take the U.S. economy off this disastrous FIRE Economy restart path that we've been on since 2001, there will be no meaningful economic recovery and no stock market recovery, only liquidity-driven rallies that respond to government reinflation policy. Every day we waste printing money and trying to reinflate a dysfunctional economic structure with taxpayer money, the more painful the eventual restructuring will be.

STOCKS AND GOLD

The stock market will keep rising through the middle part of 2010 because the markets will continue to be driven by monetary and fiscal policy in the second year of the debt deflation bear market. The Fed can't let rates rise because that will recrash the staggering, nationalized housing market and send the economy into a second recession. It can't not raise rates either, because the weak dollar will eventually lead to high oil prices that will throttle the recovery. While it copes with this contradiction, with no yield in bonds, money has two places to go in search of yield: stocks and commodities. But don't mistake price for value. Stock indexes may rise but not because the fair value of companies that make up the indexes is improving in line with the increases in stock price.

Bottom line: For most U.S. industries, the sales growth isn't there to justify stock price levels seen in early 2010. Businesses have been able to boost profits by cutting costs, but that only works for a few quarters. Payroll accounts for 70 percent of operating costs. Most of the cost reductions have come from cutting payrolls. Companies are afraid to rehire because they don't trust the recovery. The pain and expense of layoffs is still fresh in the minds of hiring managers. They'd rather increase the compensation of the employees they have and work them harder. That's why we don't see job creation while at the same time we see per-capita personal income rising, even during the recession. Just about every company I have talked to has scaled back to the bare minimum number of employees they need to operate. But as anyone who has ever run a business can tell you, if you are not growing revenues, you are failing. I expect to see another wave of bankruptcies and consolidations by 2013, when the next recession hits, induced either by austerity measures demanded of the United States by foreign lenders, or by the next oil price spike over $100 per barrel created by the next peak cheap oil cycle if lenders continue to support the United States.

The character of risks facing the markets in 2010 are not the same as those that existed in late 2007. Private credit markets have largely deleveraged between the fourth quarter of 2008 and the first quarter of 2010. Rather than find ways to restructure the bad debt left behind by thirty years of the FIRE Economy, the government has pursued policies to move bad debt from private to public account. In so doing they shifted the credit-default risk from the private to the public sector. Credit risk is now primarily sovereign risk, not private, so the next crisis event will be a sovereign debt and currency crisis.

Stocks may crash again as they did in the fall of 2008 and again in the early months of 2009, but more likely the government-financed stock market rally that began in the spring of 2009 will peter out and the indexes will go nowhere, with the Dow Jones Industrial Average drifting sideways between 9,500 and 11,000 for many years just as the NASDAQ has since 2002 and the Nikkei since 1990, while in inflation-adjusted terms the index loses 4 percent to 5 percent or more per year. The CPI number that the government issues that excludes "volatile" energy prices averaged 3.25 percent since 2004 and as of early 2010 showed a muted 2.6 percent rate. But energy price inflation has averaged 12.5 percent since 2004. Six years of steady energy price inflation, interrupted only briefly by the collapse in demand and prices during late 2008 and early 2009, contradict the assertion that energy prices are volatile and should not be included in the broad CPI measure. Energy prices are not volatile, they are rising. At some point Treasury bond holders will force the U.S. government to include energy in the CPI. When that happens interest rates will rise and Treasury bond prices will fall.

My position since 2001 is that stocks will continue to decline, and Treasury bonds and gold will continue to rise. The Treasury bond position may at first appear to contradict a gold position, because gold is widely viewed as an inflation hedge and bonds perform poorly in a high inflation environment. But I didn't buy gold in 2001 as an inflation hedge. I bought it to hedge the negative impact on the dollar of bubble reflation policies and with the expectation of dollar depreciation as unofficial antidebt deflation policy after the collapse of the technology stock bubble. The liquidity created to push bond yields down and prices up was bound to also push up commodity prices. The inverse correlation between commodity and stock prices over the past eight years will, if anything, accelerate not reverse. Gold is not like any other commodity, however, and its performance is driven by some of the factors that move commodity prices and others that are unique to gold.

Private ownership of gold is a side bet aligned with those central banks that still hold gold more than three decades after it was demonetized in the early 1970s—that is, all of the major central banks. I hold it for the same reason they do: The international political regime that supports the dollar-based system is inherently unstable and is rapidly approaching the end of its useful life span. Maybe the transition goes smoothly or maybe not. So far, not. Otherwise, why is gold holding at over $1,000?

I don't blame anyone for being afraid to buy gold near an all-time high nominal price as it was in early 2010. Rule number one of investing: Don't lose money. Rule number two: Buy cheap. But the operative word here is nominal.

When I bought gold in 2001 at $265 the metal was universally considered the worse investment you could make, and for more than the previous twenty years, it was. It was like going to a rundown ballpark of a baseball team that had been in slow decline for decades. The bleachers were 95 percent empty; only a few diehard fans, the gold bugs, remained. Paint peeled off the seats. The toilet was stopped up. The players lumbered and staggered around the field like they were on Thorazine. When on rare occasion a batter actually connected with the ball, a faint murmur arose from long-suffering fans who had grown weary of repeated failures of the team to rally. You never read about the team in the papers. It'd been written off years before.

In 2010, when gold trades over $1,100, the bleachers are nearly full, hedge fund managers and a few institutional investors mingle with the market contrarians and gold bugs. Every new price rise elicits a roar of approval from the crowd. The score appears on the front page of the *Wall Street Journal.* Now that gold is popular, does this mean its days of glory are numbered? Is gold a bubble? I've been asked that question every year since 2006, as the gold price went up from $500 to $600, $700, and $800. Every year I responded the same way: If the reasons for the price rise since 2001 remain in place, the combination of peak cheap oil and government policies to prevent debt deflation through dollar depreciation, then there is no reason why gold prices will not continue to rise.

The reluctant gold buyer did get another bite at $720 in October 2008, under the most extreme of conditions possible, when the whole world was selling anything and everything to raise cash in a panic. Unfortunately, the same fear that kept that person from buying at $700 in 2007 before the price spiked to $1,000 in 2008 probably kept them out of the gold market at $720 later that year. During the panic that pushed gold down to $720, fear had them holding off, with many market pundits calling for gold to fall to $600. A few hard-core deflationists at the time even called for gold prices to collapse as far as oil did, by 75 percent, to $250.

It's human nature to think that the day we started to notice gold beating stocks is the day that gold prices started to beat stocks. But the truth is that gold has been beating stocks for ten years. The real story of gold versus stocks since 1998 is that gold has produced better year-over-year results than stocks, and with less volatility. Here are the facts:

- The gold price has finished higher at the end than at the start of each of the last ten years, except for 2000, when gold prices fell 3 percent.
- Even in 2000, the only year over the past ten when gold prices fell, the price of gold fell less than one third as far as stocks fell.
- Gold performed worse than the S&P 500 during the stock bubble years of 1998 and 1999, when gold and stocks gained 14 percent and 23 percent, respectively. Even so, gold prices went up 1 percent in each of those years.
- The S&P 500 gave it all back and more from 2001 to 2002, when stocks fell 10 percent and 26 percent, while gold prices increased 20 percent and 17 percent.
- The S&P 500 finished higher in only six out of the past ten years.
- In three out of the four years that the S&P 500 finished lower, gold finished higher.

So far the stock market reflation rally of 2009 through 2010 is looking similar to the reflation rally of 2003, when the now famously asset-inflation happy Greenspan Fed launched the housing bubble with 1 percent interest rates and deregulation of mortgage credit. The S&P 500 shot up 23 percent that year and gold rallied 17 percent; the year after, gold rallied 20 percent and the S&P fell 26 percent.

In the first two years of that postbubble bust reflation, in 2003 and 2004, the S&P grew 3 percent net, while the gold price went up 27 percent. The "bubbles in everything" that resulted from the reflation policy produced lackluster returns on the S&P 500, while gold had three strong years between 2005 and 2008. The bubbles collapsed in 2008, with the S&P 500 down 38 percent. Even so, gold finished higher that year.

It turns out that the early 2000s reflation after the collapse of the technology stock bubble did create "bubbles in everything"—everything except gold, that is.

Gold can only be considered a refuge from calamity if by "calamity" we mean the decade-long process of credit-financed asset bubbles and collapses of the domestic FIRE Economy that, along with an equally disastrous foreign policy, resulted in a 40 percent depreciation of the dollar against major currencies.

Gold does not rise in response to future inflation fears but in response to currency risk. As the risk to the dollar has risen every year since 1998, so has gold; the greater the risk, the greater the rise.

If the United States runs out of sovereign credit before the economy becomes self-sustaining, the sovereign debt and currency event that I have warned of since 1999 may be the eventual payback for decades of FIRE Economy policies. And if that happens, not only will gold rise even more than it has nearly every year for the past decade, it may rapidly rise to the $2,500 to $5,000 range that I forecast in 2001 as the eventual gold price peak.

Some of the factors that increase dollar risk are also bullish for stocks in the short term. Near zero interest rates and heavy government borrowing to fund deficits are reinflating parts of the economy but not others. The difficulty will be in selecting which stocks benefit and which do not. We will maintain a steady discussion on the topic on iTulip.com to stay on top of trend changes as they occur.

Peak cheap oil will be a hazardously hard trend to invest in. Terminally high oil prices suggest a simple strategy to invest in oil production companies, but high and rising oil prices may not translate into high and rising oil producer profits. In fact, the opposite is more likely the case as the price that oil producers can charge for oil fails to keep up with the capital costs of finding and getting ever more difficult oil out of the ground. Oil trusts are another example of an oil investment that at first blush looks like an obvious way to make money from rising oil prices. But the value of a trust is based on the value of the oil reserves behind it. If the oil is depleting, the price of the trust is falling. It may turn out that the only viable way to invest in peak cheap oil and a weakening dollar is by investing in commodities themselves, in particular precious metals that have industrial uses, such as silver and platinum, but also agricultural commodities such as wheat.

Rules number one and two in investing are: Don't lose money and buy cheap. Locking in gains and avoiding bear markets is as important as buying cheap in the first place. It's hard to make money if you are constantly trying to make up for past losses. Don't get too attached to any asset class. Don't fall into the kind of trap the gold bugs fell into in the 1980s or stock market investors did in 1999. There will be a time to sell gold and commodities, just as there was a time to get out of the stock market in early 2000, but it's not likely to happen for many years. You can't make money watching the markets every day and trying to "beat the market" by trading on a short-term basis. The opportunity cost of frequent trading is that you can't both focus on that activity and focus on finding underpriced new investments. Spend your time trying to understand how the economy is changing and let that drive your long-term investment thesis. Look for investments that you can sit on for ten years without expending time and money on buying and selling in and out of positions. Every time you do you incur transaction costs, fees, and taxes. Your brokerage firm and the IRS will love you for it, but it's no good for your portfolio. Leave the trading to the gamblers.

SHORT GOVERNMENT

How can the United States experience inflation when unemployment is nearly 10 percent and consumer credit is contracting as it is in 2010? More people understand the "ground rule triple" rule in baseball than the nature of money creation in our hybrid fiat and exogenous credit money system. Why should they? No one ever tells them.

John Kenneth Galbraith in *Money: Whence It Came, Where It Went* wrote, "The process by which banks create money is so simple that the mind is repelled." Money borrowed into existence. The $100 credit card grocery purchase you made this week is three things at the moment that you make it. One, it is a $100 liability on your balance sheet. Two, it is a bank's $100 asset on its balance sheet. Three, it is $100 on the grocery store's cash account.

In the instant that you purchased $100 in groceries you created $100 that enters the money supply through the grocery store's cash account. That money creation was possible because of a standing agreement between two parties: you, to borrow $100, and the credit card company, to lend you $100.

That new $100 on the grocery store's cash account is then atomized. It combines with cash from a thousand similar transactions and moves from the grocery store's cash account in a series of transactions to pay invoices from suppliers, wages to employees, taxes to the government, and so on. The recipients of those transfers add the funds to their cash accounts and atomize your $100 further by making purchases with it themselves. And on and on. A tiny part of that original $100 may wind up as savings in someone's 401(k), another, part of a payment on a car, another, to make a loan.

That new $100 isn't destroyed later whether you default on the loan or repay it. Say you repay the $100 to the credit card company the month after you made the purchase. Your liability and the credit card company's asset are both canceled. But the $100 you created when you bought groceries the previous month, that was then sent in a thousand directions from the cash account of the grocery store; it floats around the economy like gas escaped into the atmosphere, continuously changing forms, forever. That $100 you created when you bought $100 in groceries never goes away. There is no reverse transaction that ties all the little atoms of the original $100 you created back into the original credit transaction that produced it. You'd have more luck collecting the atoms of carbon dioxide out of the air over Manhattan from a year-old sneeze of a tourist at the top of the Empire State Building.

A default on your credit card account doesn't destroy that money. Even if you default today on your entire credit card account, of which an unpaid $100 bill for groceries was part, from the standpoint of that $100 that was once on the grocery store's cash account, the default cancels the original transaction just as if you paid it off. The $100 you created remains in the economy. There is no magical fairy that runs around retracing each and every step of each transaction from the hundreds of accounts that engaged in transactions after the $100 was transferred off the grocery store's cash account to pay the bills.

Your default will cause your credit card company to limit credit to you by raising fees or cutting your credit limit. That reduces your ability to lend new money into existence. If millions of people like you default on credit cards at the same time, that will cause lenders to increase reserves, tighten standards, and reduce loan issuance. If at the same time unemployment rises and consumers are afraid to take on new debt, less money is borrowed into existence in aggregate. Money lent into existence through this channel of personal credit declines. A reduction in the money supply then follows indirectly from a large number of simultaneous defaults, not because the defaults on loans destroy the money that was originally created when the loan was taken out.

The money supply rises and falls as the sum of the flow of credit transactions and decisions. If more transactions repay old debt than create new debt, the money supply falls. That is what we are seeing today in the private credit markets.

For items purchased with personal credit, the decline in the money supply created by credit card loans is deflationary, but not for those purchased with other forms of credit, or cash. This brings us back to

Irving Fisher and his debt deflation theory. The general price level can be raised, and purchasing power deflated, by lowering the demand for the currency in which the debt is denominated. An economy with very high levels of inflation in fact will have a very limited market for credit. Healthy credit markets depend on low inflation rates. High inflation reduces the level of credit in an economy, not the other way around. Economies such as Argentina's, where inflation is high, are largely cash economies.

At any given time there are inflationary and deflationary forces operating in any economy, each driven by supply and demand for the goods and services and the supply and demand for the money that is used in those transactions. Monetary policy seeks to maintain a balance of these forces to prevent the development of self-reinforcing deflationary or inflationary processes, because once they develop they are costly to stop.

Central banks seek to prevent both deflation spirals, such as the one the U.S. experienced in the 1930s, and inflation spirals, like the great inflation of the late 1970s. They use various monetary tools to accomplish this. Under normal conditions we hardly notice the effects of policy changes that seek to maintain this balance. The effects are reported as aggregate price indexes, such as the consumer price index. I prefer to track the impact of policy changes using personal consumption expenditures. PCEs more accurately represent how we experience the cost mix of goods and services that results from these policies.

Under extreme conditions, monetary policies and their affects are more obvious. For example, we saw the beginnings of a second great inflation in 2008. The Fed hoped that baby-step rate hikes starting in 2004 would bring a painless end to it and give us a soft landing. But the dollar kept weakening and cost-push inflation from rising energy import prices was accelerated by hedge funds and other leveraged players bidding up the trend. The Fed was forced to raise rates to reverse the commodity price inflation trend that was due as much to the peak cheap oil cycle as it was to the weak dollar. Unfortunately for the Fed, that effort ran headlong into the asset price deflation occurring in the housing market. They thought they could avoid a crisis by raising rates slowly and with plenty of verbal warnings to entice investors out of leveraged and otherwise risky interest-rate-sensitive instruments. It didn't happen that way, and never does. The Fed never seems to learn the lesson of 1994, when the Greenspan Fed tried to pop the stock market bubble and crashed the bond markets. China's policy makers would do well to note central banks' perfect record of failure at engineering soft landings for economies that depend on housing and other asset bubbles for growth.

U.S. net capital inflows reversed in the first quarter of 2007, when foreign investors caught wind of the coming crisis. Martin Prager Mayer, banking expert and author of thirty-five nonfiction books, told me at the time, "When capital inflows reverse, watch out!" At the end of the first quarter of 2007 the market for ASB credit-default obligations crashed. The Fed immediately dropped interest rates, in a race with plunging inflation, to maintain negative real interest rates. The name of the game from there on was to prevent the asset price crash from spilling over into the real economy. The Fed's policy was crystal clear: The best way out of a liquidity trap is to not fall into one in the first place. The deflationists thought they'd lose the race. I knew they'd win and invested accordingly.

The liquidity trap that the United States fell into after the 1929 crash, and Japan's in 1992 after its 1990 crash, was not allowed to take hold in the United States in 2008. This was the policy response the Fed had promised since at least 2003. With debt levels high and incredible leverage in the banking system, the Fed had a good idea what was in store.

But it's completely unclear why they let the risks accumulate. A crisis that's predictable is preventable. If they saw the risks well enough to prepare to respond to the crisis, why didn't they instead take steps to limit the risks of a credit markets meltdown? Why not rein in the financial institutions that were creating the credit risk and prevent the crisis from occurring in the first place? That's like a doctor making extensive plans to respond to a patient's heart attack because the patient is eating cheeseburgers and milk shakes and gets no exercise. Why not prescribe a change of diet?

The Fed acts as if it has two masters. One is the financial oligarchy that influences the Fed through the New York clearing banks, and the other is its traditional base of commercial banks and financial institutions, which the Fed also attempts to serve through traditional policy channels. The Fed can operate in the interests of one constituency or the other, but rarely does the same policy work for both at the same time. For example, one of the missions of the Fed is to regulate the financial system so that risks do not accumulate that pose a systemic threat to its broader commercial banking constituency. The Fed failed to do so during the Greenspan years because the financial interests had captured its regulatory function. That conflict of interest created both the crisis and the financial sector–friendly response to the crisis.

The problem with the Fed is the people who run it and the conflicts of interest that have developed over the past thirty years. Proposals to disband the Fed are disproportionate. There are 195 countries in the world, and every one of them has some form of central bank. Are the citizens of those countries proposing legislation to rid them of their central bank? No. Why? Because it's understood that the alternatives to a central bank are even worse. Without a central bank to supply cash during financial market emergencies, a nation depends on the biggest private bankers in town. That's how we used to do it, with less than ideal results. As for price stability, if the institution responsible for managing the money supply is not at least marginally politically independent from the legislature, you can guess what happens. How'd you like Congress with one hand on the "spend" lever and the other on the "print" lever? It's bad enough as it is with the power of Congress to approve or disapprove a Fed chairman who talks a good line on economic and monetary principles but acts politically in disregard of them as in the cases of Arthur Burns and Alan Greenspan. The former oversaw the greatest commodity and wage price inflation in modern United States history in the late 1970s, the latter the greatest asset price inflations in the world from 1995 to 2006. Perhaps someday Fed central bank policy will change to view the destructive power of asset price inflation as negatively as it does the economic havoc presented by commodity and wage price inflation; it might tomorrow if only asset bubbles did not make so many bankers as rich as commodity price inflation and high interest rates makes them poor.

The fixation on the Fed is understandable, because it's easier to focus one's ire on a single entity. How do you get rid of a financial oligarchy? Getting rid of a symbol of that oligarchy is easier. The institution of the Fed needs to be reformed, not disbanded, made more independent and guided by a more rational set of policies that represent the will of the people. The public and private institutions themselves are not the root of the problem. The problem is the people running the institutions and the way they think and operate.

Since mid-2008 the U.S. government has shifted credit risk via bailouts to U.S. sovereign credit from private credit. Credit risk pollution, the term we coined in 2006 to warn our readers about the future collapse in the securitized debt market, has moved. Instead of the banks' balance sheets being polluted with risk, now the Fed and the Treasury hold the bulk of the credit risk.

No one knows exactly how that will be expressed in the markets, because no central bank has ever had a balance sheet that looks like the Fed's, with nearly half its assets in unmarketable securities, when at the same time the country ran a budget deficit in excess of 10 percent of GDP. If any other nation did the same, they'd already be paying double-digit interest rates on sovereign debt for the privilege. On the one hand we're using currency depreciation to increase inflation expectations. On the other we're flooding the markets with liquidity to hold down interest rates. We cannot keep doing both forever. Something's got to give.

Since most of the Treasury bond issuance since August 2008 is short term, the new and rapidly growing periodic issuance since June 2009 represents both a rolling over of maturing previously issued short-term Treasury debt plus brand-new issuance. Thus, the $2 trillion is not net cumulative. The total increase to the public debt from the issuance of new Treasury debt is approximately $1.7 trillion. Of that, more than one third was issued in the month of August 2009.

U.S. Treasury bonds are considered default risk–free. From 1999 until early 2001 Argentine government bonds traded at a premium to U.S. Treasury bonds. At the time, Argentina's bondholders must have believed that there was less inflation risk in Argentina than in the United States. They thought the Argentine government was more determined to manage the economy to produce low inflation and maintain the currency peg. Worst case: The IMF had their back. They were wrong on all counts. The U.S. stock market had crashed and caused an economic crisis, and the IMF abandoned Argentina. The worry today is that China is America's IMF, and may be forced to abandon the United States if an economic crisis occurs in China.

The net increase in foreign purchases of U.S. Treasury securities for the period August 2008 to August 2009 is $281 billion, approximately 20 percent of the total issuance. The balance, the other 80 percent, was purchased by domestic entities. There is plenty of circumstantial evidence about who in the United States is buying up all of these short-term Treasury bills other than U.S. households, such as commercial banks and the Fed itself, but no one really knows who all of the purchasers are and who ultimately holds what. The United States is rumored to buy through Caribbean banking centers, and Middle Eastern investors through the UK. In any case, the rate of issuance is not sustainable. I've been long on Treasury securities since 1998; in 2010, the position feels downright dangerous but the options to diversify into a safer asset are not at all obvious. Nothing is cheap, and the bonds backed by the world's largest military and political power have historically been a good bet, all other considerations aside.

THE FUTURE OF REAL ESTATE

If the FIRE Economy is down for the count, what's the future of real estate? During the transitional economy, as debt deflation hammers residential real estate prices, Americans abandon cherished fantasies, prime among them: A house is an investment. What could be more simple yet more simply wrong?

As discussed earlier, Professor Robert Shiller, in the second edition of his book *Irrational Exuberance*, demonstrated conclusively that for over one hundred years since 1990 housing prices nationally in the United States only kept up with the rate of inflation. In one hundred years there were only two exceptions. The first happened at the end of World War II. Soldiers returned home and started new families, and received government home mortgage financing under the GI Bill. The government-backed credit collided with more than a decade of pent-up demand for housing that had accumulated first during the Great Depression and then after the war. A major housing boom resulted, but not a bubble—the pent-up demand, and the demand, were real, and home prices never reverted to earlier levels.

The second exception to the rule that housing prices only rise as fast as inflation was the housing bubble that ran from 2002 until 2006.

Yet a generation of Americans, starting around the time of the early stages of the FIRE Economy in the 1970s, came to believe in a house as an investment, and in home equity as a surefire retirement savings plan. Little did they know that for the first ten years of the FIRE Economy, while the dollar cartel came together to arrange to buy oil cheap from producers in the Middle East and other nations around the globe, a five-year stretch of high inflation accounted for the apparent rapid gains in real estate. Later, starting in the early 1980s, home prices began to rise faster than inflation—asset price inflation outpaced commodity price inflation—as the FIRE Economy developed its magical specialized credit formula of inflating asset prices without inflating commodity prices and wages in the productive economy.

Most of us know someone who bought a house many years ago at a price that appears absurdly cheap today, an elderly neighbor who bought a home in the 1976 for $80,000 and sold it thirty years later for $500,000. If you were in the market for a house in 2006, on hearing such a story you may be inclined to think, "If I buy that home today for $400,000, it will be worth $2.5 million in thirty years, and I'll retire a millionaire."

But if so, you are forgetting that back in 1976, when the elderly neighbor bought the house, the prices of goods and services were proportionately lower, and that if you sell the house for six times $400,000 in thirty years, goods and services prices will be higher still. What matters when you are thinking about the prices of homes and other goods in the future is how those prices relate to your income at the same point in the future. In other words, you need to think clearly about what inflation really is and how it affects your investment decisions.

Shiller projects home prices will decline by 20 percent to 30 percent nationally for five to ten years after 2008 before resuming a normal growth rate; that is, keeping up with inflation. In some areas of the country, he expects home prices may decline 50 percent or more.

Assuming optimistically that the U.S. economy does not experience another major recession during the thirty years, that new home owners will be paying off the mortgage on their home, and that Shiller is correct that home prices will correct by a total of 20 percent and after that return to growing at the rate of inflation.

Let's shoot for the middle of Shiller's estimate and say home prices decline 20 percent in only six years, and then catch up with inflation over the remaining twenty-four years on the mortgage. At the end of thirty years, if inflation averages 3 percent, as it has officially during the FIRE Economy era, then a home will be worth $317,000.

Unfortunately, while the housing bubble set housing price appreciation—optimistically—back six years, goods and services price inflation kept chugging along. That means that the $212,000 home needs to be worth $515,000 at the end of thirty years just to break even on an inflation-adjusted basis. In this optimistic scenario, when inflation remains tame and no recessions occur for thirty years, the new home owner loses $198,000 if he buys a home in 2010—this while shelling out nearly half his income and missing out on the opportunity to invest in a portfolio of stocks and bonds that will appreciate faster than the rate of inflation.

That's bad, but unfortunately the story gets worse. Due to the weak dollar and peak cheap oil, consumer price inflation will be considerably higher over those thirty years than during the FIRE Economy or transitional economy. During the transitional economy, consumer price inflation will average 7 percent to 8 percent per year for several years, resulting in a 40 percent inflation. This period of inflation will "deflate the debt" left over from the FIRE Economy. The good news is that the $212,000 home price never falls 20 percent in the first place as Shiller expects but only about 15 percent, but the purchasing power of income declines 40 percent.

Any way you look at it, whether inflation continues at 3 percent or rises to 8 percent during the transitional economy, the housing bubble will make buying a home a losing proposition for years to come. This fact will add to a long list of grudges that generations born during the FIRE Economy era will hold against the baby-boomer generation.

One of the reasons I remain worried about the economy is the overall state of the technology start-up world. The engine of growth, new small businesses, continues to sputter, and tech start-ups are no exception. Every few days I am approached by a friend or business associate who has been unemployed or underemployed for a year or more. I see very few new businesses forming. If you are trying to start something new that requires seed capital, it is extremely hard to come by. I have friends in the VC business who are actively making new investments, but they are a rarity, and the cost of capital is ridiculous. Even for well-established companies the premoney valuation is often zero, so that entrepreneurs wind up owning only 5 percent to 10 percent of the company that the investors carve out of the stock option pool. Even companies doing $10 million or $20 million a year, if they are at a preprofit development stage, are experiencing onerous terms. Building a company from a start-up to an exit, such as an IPO or a sale, is terribly difficult even under ideal circumstances. The return on pain, the amount of money an entrepreneur can hope to earn after years of sacrifice, has never been lower. I worry that entrepreneurs will simply give up on the United States and head for greener pastures. If that happens, then the U.S. economic miracle will end.

For companies that can get financing, the money-in is the post-money valuation; that is, if the company raises $2 million, then $2 million is the valuation of the company after the company is financed. Previous investors are wiped out. These deals are structured as "pay for play," meaning the previous investors are free to participate, but basically they are starting from scratch. The new investors carve out an option pool for management and that winds up being the "ownership" that the founders get in their own company.

Most VCs continue to triage their portfolios, cutting companies that they don't think will survive and doubling down on those they think have a chance to make it to an exit. There are still some winners, but they are few and far between. Institutional funds are reducing their allocations to VC funds and private equity. The VC-financed technology industry is shrinking along with the entire U.S. economy.

I don't know why analysts have so much trouble understanding that the United States today is not the same United States we were in 1980, when the Fed raised interest rates and kept them there on purpose to create high unemployment—to take away pricing power from wage earners and cut off a wage price spiral. A net debtor who lives off capital inflows that finance domestic output, which incomes pay the taxes that back the currency, cannot behave that way. If the United States raises interest rates before the economy is growing without further stimuli, the U.S. Treasury market and dollar will fall even harder, not rise. Why? Because when our economic output is declining, our ability to service existing internal and external debt is diminished. Add high interest rates on top of that, and debt service gets even more expensive as a portion of output.

U.S. policy is to devalue the dollar gradually to reduce our $60 trillion contingent liability by half. In my opinion the dollar will be decommissioned as a primary reserve currency in that transition. Over that period—which starts now—a global reserve system based on Special Drawing Rights, or SDRs, issued by the IMF may gradually replace the dollar's current role in international trade. The IMF is positioning itself as the issuer of that reserve currency, and has for the first time issued SDR debt; it has also made reserve currency arrangements with China, Brazil, Israel, and many others. I'm not sure many observers understand the implications: countries are trying to distance themselves from the United States and protect themselves from the impact of a disorderly end to the dollar reserve regime while also trying to proceed along an orderly path to phase in an alternative. This will not be easy.

There are two major issues. Today 88 percent of all international transactions are executed in dollars. Let's say the use of SDRs grows internationally, and dollar transactions decline from 88 percent to 20 percent over the next fifteen to twenty years. At the end of the process, the United States is like any other country, earning the reserve currency through trade that it needs to conduct trade and borrowing in other currencies and SDRs. International demand for dollars for international trade falls.

According to the IMF, Russia today has US$352 billion in foreign currency reserves. India has US$261 billion. Romania has US$38 billion. The United States holds $47 billion in foreign currency reserves.

U.S. GDP is eight times greater than Russia's. The United States needs foreign currency reserves only to cover the relatively small volume of international transactions that it does not conduct in dollars. Since most countries we trade with conduct trade primarily in our currency, we don't have to maintain currency reserves to settle international transactions. This is the key advantage of issuing the world's reserve currency, an advantage that the United States wants to defend, and U.S. allies want maintained. If the world moves to SDRs, we lose that advantage. Not only that, but we can no longer issue foreign debt in our own currency. We'll be like other countries, bound by the usual constraints on trade balances and fiscal deficits. Our role as the world's demand engine and global military police force goes away because we will not be able to borrow cheaply enough to finance either activity.

We cannot depreciate our way out of debt and still retain the dollar's role as the world's reserve currency. We can't have it both ways. The end of the dollar as a primary reserve currency creates a real dilemma for the balance of global military power and the current order. The United States can't afford to act as the world's police force to maintain the status quo if it can't finance the operations of its military overseas by borrowing money from allies priced in dollars. Over the next fifteen to twenty years the United States will have to phase out its global military role. Hundreds of U.S. military bases will close over the next two decades. China and Russia's global military role will increase. You can already see the process starting in the way the international community is dealing with North Korea and Iran, and in China's display of military hardware and personnel. It is partly a show for domestic consumption, a morale booster to combat flagging confidence in the Chinese Communist Party, but it was also a message to China's trade partners that it is not only a willing and capable economic trade partner, but it can provide a security umbrella as well.

In a bipolar global power balance with the United States on one side and China on the other, an updated version of the old U.S. and Soviet world might develop over time, but a nonnational global reserve currency implies a multipolar world, not a bipolar one. Multipolar eras have in the past been periods of political instability, when old scores were settled and the aspirations of regional leaders were expressed without interference from a global hegemonic power. The implications are not very attractive when you consider the ambitions of some of the nations that are hostile to democratic capitalist systems like ours. But who knows? Maybe this time will be different.

If you are a U.S. creditor, what are you thinking? If the United States blows its debt-to-GDP ratio out to 15 percent trying to restart the FIRE Economy and fails, what then? Can we then blow it up to 25 percent of GDP trying to do it the right way?

I make my forecasts by studying the data and the history and polling people in the industry whom I've known for decades. I look for dissonance between what our insider contacts say and the data from a historical perspective. I look for the denial that I call "the desperate optimism of the invested" that typically occurs at market tops. It is a lot easier to see these events clearly as an uninvested market outsider. The paradox is that once you have made a call such as this, and if you act on it, now you too are invested in the market. The challenge going forward is to manage that and abstract yourself from events and from your own investment positions.

EPILOGUE

We must dare to think "unthinkable" thoughts. We must learn to explore all the options and possibilities that confront us in a complex and rapidly changing world. We must learn to welcome and not to fear the voices of dissent. We must dare to think about "unthinkable things," because when things become unthinkable, thinking stops and action becomes mindless.

—J. WILLIAM FULBRIGHT, MARCH 27, 1964

In this book we've confronted difficult truths about our economy. Much of our wealth and prosperity over the past three decades resulted from technological advances, the skill and training of our hardworking men and women in a thousand professions, and the application of good old American know-how. But a significant portion resulted from direct and indirect government subsidy of the finance, insurance, and real estate industries that grew at the expense of many productive industries that were once the cornerstones of American economic might.

By adopting an impractical, fundamentalist, laissez-faire ideology in the 1980s, the United States ceded economic and energy policy to investment banks. Other countries have government institutions that set national economic policy, for good or ill. Japan has its Ministry of Economy, Trade, and Industry. What we got in the United States was the FIRE Economy compliments of Wall Street. A product of an imbalance of political forces, the FIRE Economy evolved into a set of incentives to minimize saving and investment and maximize borrowing and consumption, to ship precious capital overseas in exchange for consumer goods, and to explode financial systemic risk to a level that threatened the survival of the system itself. The FIRE Economy evolved organically and, by increments, by the internal logic of our political economy, into a system more perverse than any that might be conceived of by the most devious and nefarious central planners. The result is referred to in polite circles as global imbalances.

FIRE Economy interests captured the regulatory functions of public and semipublic institutions that were developed over generations to prevent excessive risk taking by banks and investors. Deregulation and ever more competitive financial engineering forced commercial banks to take ever greater risks to compete with each other for customers and profits, and to enter markets that were formerly the arena of investment banks and hedge funds, and that operate on a completely different set of business principles—of risk and high returns, not safety and low rates of return.

For decades government-sponsored enterprises guaranteed mortgages. Tax policy allowed mortgage debt to be deducted from income. Financial deregulation encouraged the creation and sale of new mortgage debt instruments that caused an overexpansion of mortgage credit. Real estate prices grew far faster than incomes, as too much credit chased not enough houses. Rising housing values lulled home owners into believing that their homes were doing their retirement saving for them. Saving the old-fashioned way, by setting aside 8 to 10 percent of income every year in savings or 401(k) accounts, dwindled. At the same time, low interest rates and taxes on interest earned by saving encouraged households to borrow more and save less.

Industries like car manufacturing were financialized during the

FIRE Economy era as returns on financial speculation produced higher profits than returns on investment in production. One industry after another moved offshore, leaving the United States with a so-called service economy that was in fact comprised of companies that service FIRE industries that extract excessive economic rents as fees and interest from American businesses and households.

Credit risk built up in the financial system for decades. High oil prices always trigger recessions and minirecessions. Rising oil prices in 2004 caused by a combination of monetary policy, a weak dollar, and the beginning of peak cheap oil in 2004 kicked off a recession in the housing market in 2006, which led to the collapse of the securitized debt market in early 2007 and the beginning of the great recession by the end of that year. The great crash followed in 2008 as the FIRE Economy collapsed. The damage to the private credit markets spilled over into the productive economy, spurring thousands of business failures and consolidations. More than seven million jobs were lost in less than two years.

The Federal Reserve, Treasury Department, and Congress stepped in with bold and unorthodox programs to take on bad debts and unmarketable securities from banks and financial institutions. Liabilities on the Fed's balance sheet grew more in one year than in the previous ninety-five years; the composition of its assets calls into question the very solvency of the institution. Trillions—spent to bail out banks and insurance companies, prop up the collapsed housing market, and keep afloat struggling giants like General Motors that employ hundreds of thousands—have put the nation's already wobbly finances in a league with third world countries.

The collapsed FIRE Economy era leaves a legacy of trillions of dollars of private sector debt that eats away at the pillars of the productive economy that were not displaced by the finance, insurance, and real estate industries during this period. In 2007 the United States experienced a balance-sheet recession, so called because the economy drifts in and out of recession as households and businesses fix their balance sheets—specifically, old debts. Japan has been experiencing this lesson since the early 1990s. Cash flows from households and business are diverted toward debt repayment, with loan payments going to repay huge mortgages on inflated home prices rather than toward saving and investment for future growth.

Economic growth now depends on continuous support from the government: on public policy to move bad private debts from the accounts of banks to public account—onto the books of the U.S. Treasury and the Federal Reserve—through programs to buy bad debts and unmarketable assets; government spending programs to "create employment" and generate the income to pay the old debt promises to expand the public debt even further. Eventually, if this course is pursued to its logical conclusion, the United States will run out of credit and experience a sovereign credit and dollar crisis.

Besides crowding out productive industry and leaving behind mountains of debt, the FIRE Economy also created gigantic disparities of wealth, debt, and income. These didn't matter when the economic pie was growing, but as the economy stagnates, unemployment remains stubbornly high, and the economic pie first stops growing and then shrinks, these disparities will become a major political issue. Populist politicians will offer unconstructive solutions that appear to solve short-term crises but in the long run lay the foundations for one crisis after another. No crisis will be more dire, and exert economic pain less evenly, than the onset of permanently high and rising oil prices that act like a regressive tax that consumes an ever-greater portion of the incomes of the lowest-earning households.

The dollar cartel allowed the United States and its allies to buy oil at artificially low prices by overvaluing the dollar. Oil was consumed at below market prices, motivating the United States to underconserve and creating incentives for oil producers to overproduce. After more than thirty years the United States is left with one of the most energy-intensive economies in the world.

The first wave of oil price increases caused by both a peak in global oil production and the phasing out, or possible collapse, of the dollar cartel bears down on the United States. These events will cause the dollar price of oil to rise in a series of sharp price spikes that will cause major new economic recessions over the next ten years—the peak cheap oil cycle—leading to even greater government expenditures to try to cushion the impact on the population, especially on those of modest means.

During the FIRE Economy years, the United States took a joyride on an ocean of cheap oil that, in the absence of any rational energy policy, allowed the United States to build one of the world's most inefficient transportation systems. Lack of transportation energy policy culminated in the penultimate symbol of energy waste and extravagance, GM's Hummer, now a division of the Chinese truck manufacturer Sichuan Tengzhong Heavy Industrial Machinery Company, after the economic crisis forced GM to sell the brand in June 2009.

How can the United States cope with the end of the collapse of the FIRE Economy and the onset of the peak cheap oil? How can the United States finance a restructuring of its economy around production, saving, and investment when so much money and credit has already been expended in a vain effort to get the credit bubble machine going again?

I've argued in this book that the United States must return to its roots, as the world's leading creative inventor, saver, and investor, and use the rapidly approaching energy emergency as a political forcing function to unleash the entrepreneurial engine of growth to develop the transportation, energy, and communications infrastructure we need to ensure the nation's future competitiveness. We all must work to phase out the FIRE Economy and develop the TECI Economy.

Every dollar wasted in a hopeless effort to restart the wasteful and unsustainable FIRE Economy is a dollar we won't have to invest in the TECI Economy—a dollar we won't have to make America solvent and competitive. Remove the government subsidies of unproductive industries and use the tax revenue generated to finance investment in the TECI Economy. Enforce existing financial regulations so that finance once again *serves* the productive economy instead of rules it. Deploy private capital with government participation in public-private partnerships to major projects to improve public transportation, upgrade the electricity grid, and build out nuclear power plants to reduce dependence on fossil fuels of all kinds. Open venture capital investment to a wider range of investors to increase the pool of capital available to finance companies that build TECI Economy project feeder technologies, from nanotech to biotech to broadband wireless communications. None of this is easy, none is an easy sell. But all of it is necessary.

The next ten years will be the most challenging for the United States since World War II. It is exactly the kind of emergency that mobilizes America's greatest virtues, of get-it-done practicality, of creative problem solving, but also of the ideals of fairness and honor, of decency and rule of law, of community, equality, and opportunity. Soon circumstances will arise that demand us to show who we are as a people. I have no doubt that we will rise to it and show the world once again what America is about.

ACKNOWLEDGMENTS

—

You could say this book was instigated by *Harper's Magazine* editor Paul Ford, who contacted me after my Web site iTulip.com republished a prescient May 2006 *Harper's* article by professor Michael Hudson titled "New Road to Serfdom: An Illustrated Guide to the Coming Real Estate Collapse."

The article laid out the housing bubble carnage to come in precise detail. The title is a takeoff of Friedrich von Hayek's influential and popular exposition of classical liberalism and libertarianism, *The Road to Serfdom*, published in 1944. Hudson's case: neo-libertarianism closed the door on the state at least so far as preventing the heavy hand of government from invading the personal lives of Americans with excessive taxation. But a political economy thus organized left a back door open for banks, insurance companies, and other financial interests to invade every corner of American life, to levy economic rents on housing, education, health care, and other essentials as interest payments on debt, transaction fees, and the like.

Hudson begins the article with a quotation from H. G. Wells's 1936 *The Shape of Things to Come*: "Even men who were engaged in organizing debt-serf cultivation and debt-serf industrialism in the American cotton districts, in the old rubber plantations, and in the factories of India, China, and southern Italy, appeared as generous supporters of and subscribers to the sacred cause of individual liberty." In a triumph of ideology over common sense, millions of Americans, by the mundane act of buying a mortgage during the housing bubble, entered willingly into a modern form of financial debt-serf cultivation sold to them as the American dream of home ownership.

That contact by Paul developed into my writing the March 2008 *Harper's* cover article, "The Next Bubble," which led me to professor Michael Hudson himself. I owe Michael a special debt of gratitude for revealing the existence of an economy based on finance, insurance, and real estate that has come to be known as the FIRE Economy, for his unique grasp of finance from his days at Morgan Chase, for his encyclopedic knowledge of economic history, and for his unique expertise in the minutiae of the Fed Flow of Funds and NIPA reports that inform a data-driven understanding of how the U.S. economy actually works.

While he and I may not always agree on solutions, Michael's scholarly critique of finance capitalism in defense of industrial capitalism accords with my heartfelt desire to see my great country phase out the latter in pursuit of policies of neo-industrial development. The *Harper's* article caught the attention of literary agent Ted Weinstein, whom I had to good fortune to sign on with, and without whose steady guidance, advocacy, and occasional stern prodding, this book would not have seen the light of day.

If not for Ted I'd never have met my publisher, Adrian Zackheim at Portfolio Penguin, whose vision and personal conviction made this book possible.

My good fortune continued with the assignment by Adrian of my editor David Moldawer, whose tireless attention to a thousand details and decisions gives the book its quality of completeness and professionalism. I am also grateful to my developmental editor Tim Sullivan, who helped me assemble the book from a collection of ideas into a consistent whole.

If Paul was the instigator, then the foundation of this book is the iTulip.com community and its thousands of members who hail from over seventy countries and span hundreds of professions—from ER doctors to energy executives to hedge fund managers to commodity traders, each contributing his or her own unique expertise and global perspective, often critical but always respectful. They are a bottomless well of inspiration, ideas, sources, and thoughtful critique. No weakly argued or poorly documented assertion gets by this crew, but data-driven, ideology-free analysis is warmly greeted there. It is in this engaging crucible of ideas that many of the concepts expressed in this book were formed. Among the thousands of iTulip community members, sixty stand out as our most active, enduring, and perceptive contributors and I salute you here: *T*, Andreuccio , ASH, babbittd, bart, bill, BiscayneSunrise, blazespinnaker, c1ue, Charles Mackay, Chomsky, Chris, Chris Coles, cjppjc, cobben, D-Mack, DemonD, don, doom&gloom, dummass (who is anything but), Finster, flintlock, goadam1, grapejelly, GRG55, hayekvindicated, icm63, Jay, Jim Nickerson, jimmygu3, jk, jpatter666, jtabeb, LargoWinch, marvenger, Master Shake, Mega, metalman, phirang, rabot10, raja, Rajiv, Raz, rjwjr, santafe2, Sapiens (may he rest in peace), Sharky, Spartacus, Starving Steve, sunskyfan, $#* (aka Symbols), The Outback Oracle, ThePythonic Cow, touchring, Tulpen, WDCRob, we_are_toast, WildspitzE, and zoog.

If iTulip.com and its community are the engine of this book, then my friend and former CEO of Media 100 John Molinari is the spark that got iTulip going again in March 2006 after a five-year hiatus. He implored me to not run another venture capital–backed company back in early 2006, but rather turn iTulip.com into iTulip, Inc. It was the right advice at the right time and I shall be forever grateful.

I am also indebted to the dozens of interviewees who generously gave their time to be interviewed either for the book or for iTulip.com, including Dean Baker, John Challenger, Jim Finkel, Mason Gaffney, Louis-Vincent Gave, Steve Keen, Christina Lampe-Onnerud, Martin Mayer, Dror Oved, Udi Melrav, Jim Rogers, James D. Scurlock, Janet Tavakoli, Dr. Peter Warburton, Elizabeth Warren, and Ronald C. Ward.

ACKNOWLEDGMENTS

—

The dozens of others who agreed to be interviewed off the record cannot be named, but I appreciate their contributions no less.

I gratefully acknowledge the support of the community of finance and economics writers and bloggers who have tirelessly fought back the tide of disinformation during the bubble era, including John Rubino of dollarcollapse.com, Mike (Mish) Shedlock of globaleconomicanalysis. blogspot.com, Barry Ritholtz of bigpicture.typepad.com, Jesse of jessescrossroadscafe.blogspot.com, and Paul Farrell of marketwatch.com.

I'd like to give a special note of thanks to my dear old friend David Weisman, whom I met at Stratus Computer twenty-seven years ago and who has since then helped me in more ways than he knows to think creatively about economics and finance.

But none of it—the book, iTulip.com, and my nearly two decades of experience as an executive and entrepreneur in the technology and finance industries that inform my views—could have happened without my wife Candy, who is thoughtfulness, wisdom, and care personified. This book was not written once since 2008 but three or four times, and while I worked on it and kept my day job, Candy held everything else together. I cannot image how this book and all that came before could have happened without her love.

INDEX

—